REALITY
AND
ECSTASY

REALITY
AND
ECSTASY

A RELIGION FOR THE 21ST CENTURY

HARVEY SEIFERT

THE WESTMINSTER PRESS · PHILADELPHIA

PUBLISHED BY THE WESTMINSTER PRESS ®
PHILADELPHIA, PENNSYLVANIA

PRINTED IN THE UNITED STATES OF AMERICA

Library of Congress Cataloging in Publication Data

Seifert, Harvey.
   Reality and ecstasy.

   Includes bibliographical references.
   1. Religion.   I. Title.
BL48.S43   200'.9   74-9713
ISBN 0-664-24990-6

CONTENTS

PREFACE

This is a book for those who, in spite of our defections and disasters, are impressed with the possibilities in human life and who want to check out what religion has to offer in a scintillating new world. Whatever religion may have contributed in the past, how can it possibly keep up with the catapulting changes in contemporary culture?

This book is especially for those on the edges of organized religious groups—either on the inside looking out or on the outside looking in. There are many such people. Research suggests that a majority of people inside many churches are raising serious questions about what their group teaches and does, and even occasionally wonder whether they should withdraw. At the same time many people outside the church are now developing a vast

interest in the possibilities in religion. With nos-
talgia, wistfulness, or curiosity, they are looking for
an expression of religion they could honestly and
helpfully become a part of.

Exploring a religion adequate for the future
means raising basic questions. What can we believe if we want knowledge solidly rooted in reality? How can religious experience provide supra-
ecstasy, even during our most dismal moments?
How does the comprehensive view of religion help
us through the complex accumulation of social
problems that now threatens our existence? What
is promising or repelling about churches, syna-
gogues, or temples? How may we add all this up in
a way that relates the whole person to the whole of
reality? On these matters there is a great ferment of
novel resources in both religion and the human
sciences. That is what these pages are about.

If the use of "21st Century" in the title seems
presumptuous to you, it does to me too. In times of
rapid change, who can speak now of the middle of
the next century? But from the perspective of the
sociology of religion we can speak of current
trends and directions for change that will be essential for entering the twenty-first century with any
degree of zest and promise.

Even that more modest aim would have been
unthinkable without much help, here gratefully acknowledged, from the many laypersons and
groups, inside and outside the church, with whom
I have discussed this material, from many students
and colleagues, especially John B. Cobb, Jr., and
Dan D. Rhoades for reading portions of an early

draft, and from my wife, Lois, for more than could be mentioned on several pages of preface.

H.S.

School of Theology at Claremont
Claremont, California

1

COLLISION WITH REALITY

Fortunately the prevailing religions of the past are no longer acceptable to modern generations. We are busy doing in religion what we are doing in other dimensions of human life—bursting the bonds of former inadequacies. During these years of our approach to the twenty-first century, populations are remarkable both for their opposition to and their interest in religion. Simultaneously there is a softening of support for religious organizations and a resurgence of active search for religious resources. A widespread questioning of and questing for religion suggests a strong desire for a more adequate religion. Most people in this country are interested in religion, but often not in the kind of religion that is being promoted by most of our churches.

We are waking up to the fact that life could be continuously happy and exciting. Yet for many, existence is still dismal and dull. Janis Joplin said, shortly before her premature death from drugs, "I'll feel better in hell." But it is possible to explode into life instead of sleepwalking toward death. We are also breaking through into reality when we see that we no longer have to tolerate war or pollution or exploitation. There are other options. Whether we actually will do so or not, we *could* do much better than any previous generation. We know more about the physical world, about human institutions, and about how to achieve goals. Yet our priorities for action have not kept up with available knowledge. This is the kind of imbalance of commitments with which religion can deal, provided that advancements in religion are rapid enough to keep up with accelerated change in the other aspects of our existence. Ancient religions unchanged are no more satisfactory for modern life than communicating by smoke signals or learning physics from a fourteenth-century textbook.

Fortunately we can improve upon our ancestors. Not only are theology and Biblical studies better equipped than ever before but newer disciplines such as the psychology and the sociology of religion are rapidly developing as allies in discovery. Historical insights are still as important in religion as in science. Some discoveries by our ancestors were more adequate, basic, and permanent than others. The general shape of the wheel has not been modified much, but calculating machines certainly have changed, from fingers to computers. We can be grateful that religion has long historical roots. We can also rejoice that it is the nature of valid religion to change, since religion always calls for concentration on something more perfect, still ahead and unrealized. Among those alert to such matters there is a widespread feeling, as Rocco Caporale puts it, that "something qualitatively new and unprecedented is happening to religion in contemporary society." [1]

Our experience can be comparable to that of the explorer who climbed an unknown peak for his first view of the Pacific—or a future researcher who has his first look at the summary figures that indicate he has found an effective cure for cancer. Already possible is a similar experience of realizing that religious resources can liberate unsuspected powers in persons for an unimaginably superior existence, and that those resources can point sure directions toward a society of unprecedented peace, justice, and opportunity.

Most of the population—including substantial numbers inside churches—know very little about these comparatively recent developments. It is time they found out. Trapped in trivia and with basic contradictions tearing us apart, we need the total wholeness within and the inclusive unity without that has become the increasing capability of religion. While global disasters move closer, we are still using tragically tiny portions of our total human potentialities. We had better learn quickly the astonishing liberation which is possible from a joining of theology to the natural, psychological, and social sciences.

In all this I am speaking of religion as a way of life shaped by the highest we can know. The religious person takes seriously in his personal life a dimension of reality which is more whole, ultimate, or unachieved, and which transforms every other aspect of existence. Religion goes beyond ordinarily accepted and limited commitments to concerns so comprehensive, thoroughgoing, and ultimate as to set the course of life in new directions.

As will be elaborated in later chapters, such a life-style is much more than a set of beliefs. But in view of our commendable clamoring for credibility, it may be well to begin with a discussion of bases for religious belief. In unfolding the possibilities in a religion for the future, this chapter will suggest that the essential beliefs of high religion have as satisfactorily solid foundations as do other complex aspects of human knowledge on which we quite willingly build our lives. Stressing these more credible foundations does indeed require considerable change from the past emphases of many religious groups, but this change is already well under way.

The Collapse of Traditional Authorities

There is still a considerable reservoir of public gullibility, which allows us to increase sales by attractive packaging, or to elect presidents by the same strategies we use to sell dog food, or to build congregations around even the most fantastic religious nonsense. Fortunately, however, recent generations demand significantly more convincing verification for what they believe about religion or anything else. Fortunately also, we have ways of discovering truth about reality that were not available in earlier times. The combination of sophisticated skepticism and exploratory expertise should make possible a more solid base for popular faith.

It is no longer convincing to appeal to prestigious persons as authorities. Insofar as we have access to other data that we consider reliable, we do not hesitate to question even the "experts." Politicians are often discredited, and even scientists are suspected of preparing for disaster. Parents, professors, and popes are all seen as fallible. We have observed very prestigious people keeping their mouths wide open, and their eyes, ears, and brains tight shut. We are quite willing to say about some modern elites, "There is no truth in their mouth; their heart is destruction, their throat is an open sepulchre, they flatter with their tongue" (Ps. 5:9).

Even the collective authority of long-established custom is suspect. To be sure, we still want to be well thought of by our peers. Anthropologists show how in various times and places this concern has been a powerful pressure, moving people toward adding fresh skulls to their collection or lending their wives to a guest or keeping their lawns well trimmed. Other-directed persons tend to invest custom with ultimate authority, adopting a Gallup Poll ethic or a Kinsey Report morality. Yet in our pluralistic times we also recognize the dangers in many of our social habits and pressures to conform. Dueling, the burning of widows, and indiscriminate slaughtering of the enemy have all been sanctioned by custom. When there are glaring social inadequacies, enforcing custom is comparable to tubercular people seeking health by coughing into each other's faces.

The appeal to history is also becoming highly suspect. The fact that an idea has been accepted for a long time does indicate enough appeal to impress many people. To this extent it needs to be taken seriously. On the other hand, the longer an idea has been accepted, the more likely it is that we should now be able to improve upon it. Neither antiquity nor modernity is a convincing proof of truth. Any generation is foolish if it does not hold to tradition until something better is found. Holidays from history and amnesia about the past are dangerous and inefficient. It is often better to flick the switch on the wall than to insist on repeating for oneself the thousands of experiments Edison performed in discovering the electric light. On the other hand, it is about time we refused to continue long-established patterns of squeezing the trigger on guns or bomb mechanisms in senseless wars. It is true that he who does not learn from history is condemned to repeat all the mistakes of history. It is also true that he who never goes beyond history will have no improved future. Anyone who believes in dynamic movement knows that the present conventional version is never the complete truth. As Karl Barth expressed it, history is not our grave, but our cradle. Progress depends upon disbelieving historical formulations and shaking loose from the tyranny of custom. Since we now live under the "future shock" of rapid change, we are more likely to regard historical ways as inadequate. Understandably, this makes the teachings of religion suspect insofar as religion often appears to be the only major human enterprise that looks backward for its most authoritative statements.

Contemporary skepticism includes rejection of the inherent authority of the Bible as such. Fewer and fewer people are responding positively to the preacher's argument, "The Bible says . . . ." More and more people are aware of outdated parts of the Bible, such as demon possession and subordination of women, for example, and they have not developed a way of sorting out the false from the true. Many of us have yet to learn that, far from being antireligious, a critical attitude toward both past and present emerges from the very heart of high religious faith itself. Every historical formulation is to be suspected in the light of a more infinite and ultimate whole. To accept as final the authority of any human organization or tradition or book is to give first allegiance to an idol rather than to the God of truth who transcends every thought and act of humankind.

In our day, intuition is also coming off badly as a reliable source for truth. I am using "intuition" to mean the immediate acceptance of a conclusion without checking it against other evidence. The proposition is considered self-validating without any other confirming experience. The assurance of

untested subjective certainty is considered to be
enough, whether it be the feeling that I should
phone a friend, bet on a horse, or believe in prayer.
The word "revelation" has often been used in this
sense. (It will be seen later that the word can also
be used with other meanings.) Men have worked
hard or enslaved others to work for them, they
have died or killed, simply because they uncritically and with immediacy felt this to be the will
of God. Insofar as they thought of revelation in this
self-validating way, they made no serious attempt
to test their conviction by further data or reflection
or deduction from any other propositions.

There is some place for the intuitional approach,
but only because there are situations in which we
cannot appeal to a better method. There are un-
proved fundamental postulates in all knowledge,
including the most rigorous of the sciences. These
irreducible presuppositions include, for example,
the reality of the self or the discoverability and the
desirability of knowledge. Or we trust the feel of
our fingers or the message in our eyes, though
these impressions and the entire system built on
them might be quite illusory. There is some evidence to support these presuppositions, and they
seem to work out in practice. But it is always possible that other assumptions would work out even
better. These basic propositions still involve a leap
of faith.

Furthermore, a hypothesis or conclusion is likely
to embody elements not included in the original
data or in any available evidence. Originality, creativity, and imagination are essential to discovery.

Insofar as intuition is imagination informed by memory, it may be an important stage in the formation of belief. Fuller testing comes later. Scientists have made great imaginative leaps of conjecture at the most novel and critical points of advance for human knowledge, as in the theory of relativity. Applying the principles of foreign policy to a new situation always involves risky ventures. Intuition akin to that of an artist is part of the equipment of the statesman. The leap of faith that is being made may be in the direction in which evidence points, but it is still an expression of faith. Two men were looking out of the train window at a flock of sheep. One said, "Those sheep have been shorn." The other more exactingly replied, "Well, at least on this side."

Because some things cannot be fully tested, a great deal of intuitive material inevitably remains in any belief system. Yet there are also dangerous weaknesses in intuitional conclusions. If we do not go beyond intuition to some kind of appeal to another source of evidence, we have no way of handling contradictions within individual belief systems or between different persons. Without such additional tests, devotees of the Koran or the Book of Mormon or *The Farmer's Almanac* have just as much claim to correctness of their self-validating awareness as does the believer in the Bible. Republicans, Democrats, or Communists are then doomed to a permanent stand-off. Self-validating intuitions can only be asserted and accepted. They are not matters for debate or further validation. Antagonists have no way of convincing each other ex-

cept by shouting " 'tis," " 'tisn't" like petulant children. Unfortunately this kind of shrill screaming
can be heard on any kindergarten playground or in
the halls of the United Nations building.

Intuition is easily tied to emotional rigidity and
fanaticism. As Edgar Brightman once put it, reliance on intuition leaves us prey to "unchecked in-
coherence and unbridled fanaticism." Claims to
special revelation have repeatedly been associated
with theological dogmatism, closed-minded big-
otry, and diabolical cruelty.

Furthermore, self-validating awareness is likely
to be socially conservative and to support what we
are now doing or have been doing in the past. The
psychology and the sociology of knowledge help
us here. As persons with deeply rooted desires, we
believe what we want to believe. We also tend to
believe what is acceptable in our society. We easily conclude that God wills what we want to do, or
that the force of the universe is on the side of what
our society defines as "good." The American is
more likely to feel spontaneously that the American way is best. Even a saintly bishop finds it hard
to believe that God wants him to give up his special ecclesiastical authority. Reliance on intuition
easily becomes a way of preserving existing forms
of domination, either by the subconscious or by society.

Flashes of insight, mystical feelings, imaginative
projections are all important. They become dangerous only when accepted uncritically without the
use of such other tests as are available. Beliefs
about a flat earth should have been labeled as false

superstitions after man's first voyage sailing west which brought him out in the east. In a complex matter such as relieving poverty, unaided intuition does not inform us accurately what would happen to the poor if we passed a minimum wage law or raised the interest rates of the Federal Reserve system. Ignorant love spawns immoral action. To remain content with such ignorance is to limit our abilities, to glorify incompetence, and to produce unintended consequences.

Gandhi cultivated the habit of making his inner voice "hold its breath" for a while to give him time to consider other factors. Unquestioned acceptance of intuition is to be kept to a minimum. Instead of broadening the area for acceptance of pure intuition to include as much as possible, this area ought to be narrowed to as little as necessary. Wherever possible, intuitions are to be tested by more reliable sources of knowledge. Leaps of faith may need to go beyond presently available evidence, but they ought to be made in the direction in which that evidence points.

Vast numbers of modern persons insist upon this. They no longer accept the prime authority of tradition, of the Bible, and of revelation. Yet in the past these often have been the chief reliances of religious proclamation. This has been a major cause of modern alienation from the church. There is increasingly little response to a religion that insists on blind acceptance. Most of us believe that action unsupported by evidence is as ineffective as an umbrella in a tornado.

It is true that in a reaction against extremist

scientism, a considerable number today are questioning some conventional ways of accumulating evidence. There has been a flurry of interest in astrology or in similar esoteric or erratic methods. The number of persons so infatuated can be greatly exaggerated in the mass media. It is still the exceptional "Man bites dog" that is considered news, instead of the much more frequent "Dog bites man." This makes it hard to determine trends from newspapers. Journalistic sociology can be quite misleading. Besides, even those who rebel against the rational accumulation of evidence still make by far the most of their daily decisions by the basic scientific methods they claim to reject. In walking they keep putting one foot down after the other because historical experience suggests that the solid earth is still likely to be there. Observation and experience rationally interpreted do inform them about how to build a house or fry an egg or plant an organic garden. Every time they use a meaningful sentence they pay tribute to the desirability of logical coherence. No meaning is communicated by incoherent language such as, "A barefoot boy with shoes on stood sitting in the liquid grass."

There are also those today who are so indecisive that they seem willing to accept almost any view. They resist coming to conclusions and rest easily with conflicting interpretations. Whatever feels right to anyone is to be accepted by others. Each individual is considered the artist of his own identity, but largely on the basis of purely personal experience and preference, with little regard for other historical or contemporary evidence. Such pluralism or subjectivism or relativism has something to be said for it, up to a limited point. On some specific cultural matters, such as preferences for classical or atonal music, or for German or Vietnamese cuisine, we may well cultivate variety on the basis of personal preference. But our nation cannot simultaneously have two foreign policies toward China. Or if one wants to land a space capsule near the recovery ship instead of crashing it into Mt. Whitney, it becomes crucial to choose precisely between thirty or thirty-one seconds' duration of motor thrust. We cannot have these things both ways. The basic characteristics of physical reality and of group life fix limits within which individual preferences can operate at any given time. Joan Miró, known for the spontaneous novelty of his painting, also deemphasizes the role of the irrational. "It is essential," he says, "to have your feet firmly planted in order to leap in the air." [2]

If it is to cope constructively with our basic crises, the religion of the twenty-first century will move beyond the mood of relativistic, irrational noncommitment to comprehensively grounded conviction, along with pluralism in those areas in which it is appropriate in the nature of things. Like the general population, those who show up at church on Sunday morning increasingly ask for variety where that is desirable. They also increasingly want religious faith grounded on acceptable evidence. When asked to pray that there is no health in us, laypersons may well wish that liturgists were acquainted with psychological evidence to the contrary. Parishioners may have con-

siderably greater confidence in the chart projected
for a satellite's orbit than they do in a so-called
Biblical scheme of the fall of man and the resulting
plan of salvation. We are becoming less likely to
accept a religion that rests on untested or contradictory grounds. Any religious interpretation to be
widely adopted must meet tests of truth similar to
those used for other accepted knowledge.

Reality-based Religion

Truth is that which corresponds with reality. It
describes things as they really are. Insofar as at all
possible, we base our conclusions on reality-
exploring procedures. These apply tests of (1) cor-
respondence with reality, (2) validating consequences as they are tried out in the existing world,
and (3) coherence with all else that we know about
other aspects of reality. Most of us tend to agree
that the best procedure is to collect all available
relevant information, classify and compare it, explore further where necessary to fill gaps or to reduce major contradictions, come to a tentative conclusion that "makes sense," try it out, and modify it
in the light of results or additional evidence. This
is the general method commonly approved for believing whatever we believe. The appeal is to systematic observation, rational interpretation, and reality testing. We gather data through experience
and we rationally interpret its meaning. This approach may be called the empirical or scientific
method, if both those terms are used in their
broader senses. It is this method which we basi-

cally have confidence in when we plan a vacation itinerary, build a bridge, study frogs, choose between two jobs, or vote for a candidate for Congress.

This method should cause no problem for religion. This is what religion is all about—basing life on a comprehensive interpretation of reality. If this general empirical process is adopted in religion, we can have the same sound basis for religious belief that we have for established conclusions in other areas of human interest. We can then assert religious truths with the same kind of confidence we give to findings of the physical and social sciences. In religion also we can arrive at conclusions solid enough to build life on. The most responsible interpreters of religion today are not trying to defend strange tales let down by miraculous skyhooks on tables of stone or tablets of gold. The fact that religious persons did this in the past seems just as strange to modern theologians as alchemy seems to present-day chemists. Reality-based religious persons today are rejecting self-validating intuitions and are insisting on comprehensively observing the full range of data, rationally interpreting it, and experimentally modifying or validating the resulting descriptions of reality. Conclusions based on this process can be convincingly communicated to modern, scientifically oriented generations.

At the same time that there is an underlying continuity in method, there are significant differences between degrees of certainty in the physical, social, and religious sciences. As one moves from the physical sciences to the social sciences, the material for study becomes more complex and less controllable. Men and women cannot be put into test tubes for experimentation. The factors that lead an adolescent to delinquency or that elect an American President cannot be precisely weighed and compared. When we move from the social sciences to philosophy and religion, we take still another step toward complexity and away from controllability.

We therefore use the particular empirical methods that are most appropriate to the field of investigation. We may move from the microscope in biology to depth interviews in psychology to rational reflection in philosophy. I believe that Jane has red hair or that there are rocks in my garden because of direct sense experience. The supposition that there was once volcanic action on the moon involves more inference and a greater leap of faith. That a particular foreign policy is best or that a specific approach to inflation control should be legislated has less conclusive supporting evidence. If we ask, "Is it raining?" we can look out of the window to see. When we explore the reliability of mystical experience, however, things get more complicated. The list of methods then to be used might include a variety of procedures from the social and psychological sciences, philosophical analysis, or the study of comparative religious experience.

As we move from the physical to the social to the religious sciences, it becomes less possible to arrive at conclusive proof of one's beliefs. At the

same time, these differences can easily be exaggerated. Actually, there is not so wide a spread as we
often suppose. Not only can theology have a more
empirical base than we think, but physical scientists make more assumptions than we commonly
suppose. Physical science establishes something
less than certainty, and theology establishes something more than credibility.

Even the physical scientist is not so certain
about the adequacy of his observations. All physical and social observations are filtered through persons with biases shaped by previous experience.
The mind of the observer always interprets, putting something of itself into what is experienced.
Anthropologists, for example, may completely mis-
interpret some aspects of a primitive culture because they continue to look at it through alien categories. Even direct sense perceptions may not
reflect things as they really are. A straight stick entering the water looks crooked. We do not really
see stars, but only the light that left them long
years ago. Human eyes do not see the entire spectrum, nor do human ears hear all wavelengths. In
dealing with the far reaches of time, we are like in-
sects with a three-week life-span who can never
experience all the four seasons in a fifty-two-week
year. They experience either the snows of winter
or the intense heat of summer, and without communication must conclude that reality is always
like that. Man is similarly handicapped when he
talks about the future or about the origin of things.

Furthermore, our position as observers alters
what we see. For some kinds of phenomena, the

very methods we must use in observation change what is observed. We never see some nuclear particles, for example, in their unobserved and undisturbed state. When researchers move in to study workers in a factory, the very presence of the investigators changes the way the employees work. Even physical scientists recognize that their measurements are never completely exact. In a sense, each observation is a deception, since the best we can do is merely approximate reality. There is further distortion when impressions are reported in language—a set of symbols that is never a complete reflection of what is intended. Careful modern scientists recognize that they are dealing not with certainties but with probabilities. Bertrand Russell has been quoted as saying, "In mathematics we never know what we are talking about, or whether what we say is true or not, but it is the most certain of all our knowledge." A meticulous scientist can never be contemptuous of faith, for the very sound reason that faith is always an unavoidable ingredient in his own scientific process.

Although the differences are not so great as commonly supposed, still, as we move from physical to social to religious inquiry, conclusions do become somewhat more difficult to sustain. At the same time, as we move from physical to social to spiritual, the issues also become more crucial. What is the moral capacity of man? What is the good life? Is there a God? These questions are comprehensive, seeking a view of the whole of things. They are basic to all other questions we raise. To live at all satisfactorily we must take a position on these ultimate issues. These answers are essential to the best life, personally and socially. With such decisive and basic importance tied to the issues involved, in religion of all areas we must certainly do what we do in other fields, namely, gather all available evidence and act on the probabilities we have.

In all these fields we do have sufficient evidence for confidence. Research methodology has developed safeguards against possible distortions of reality. Scientific measurements may be only approximate, but they are close enough to land a returning moonship within a mile of its target, or to manufacture intricate and tiny transistors, or to cure long-resistant diseases. We do have enough resources in science and theology to develop our potentialities as human beings, to find spiritual fulfillment, and to make the difference between continuation or disappearance of the human race. In religion we do have a solid enough basis that we can build our lives on it. Like all other knowledge, religious faith is not believing the unbelievable, but moving in the direction the evidence points.

Moral demands, for example, can be soundly based on the nature of reality. The goals we project as desirable for the future are informed by the long experience of the past. The imperative ("what ought to be") can be based on the declarative ("what is"). If we use up scarce natural resources, there will be none for the next generation. Or, if we act lovingly and cooperatively, we have found that we can liberate and reinforce each other's capacities. If a group of persons with normal human needs set out to start a completely new society on an isolated island, many of our common standards would soon come trooping back again. If during the first night someone ran away with the food supply, we would begin talking about some sort of regulation against stealing. When unwashed dishes accumulate in a commune—or worse, when meals are no longer being prepared—there is likely to be a growing sentiment for accepting common work standards. Just as it is necessary to eat or to die, to breathe air or to suffocate, so it is also necessary to love or to remain a pinched personality. This is the nature of reality. Instead of saying "Be good," we could say "Be realistic," or "Don't be stupid."

A similar basis in reality can also be found for theological statements. Indeed, theological reflection can no longer reliably take place apart from the natural and behavioral sciences. Theology needs to go to school with sociology, psychology, history, biology, physics, astronomy, and other such disciplines. How can we speak adequately about the nature of man without psychology, or of the character of God without observing the natural world? On the other hand, we can know neither the nature of man nor the character of God without raising more questions than psychologists and physicists normally raise.

Unscientific Uses of Science

A consistent loyalty to the empirical method requires a full survey of the whole of things, including ethical and religious factors. If those com-

mitted to scientific inquiry omit such issues, they
are not being true to their own preferred method.
When they do not take into account large sections
of reality, scientists are not being scientific
enough. Attempting to solve comprehensive problems on this partial basis is like trying to find one's
way from Reno to Rome with only a road map of
Iowa.

We miss essential facts when we do not raise the
more ultimate questions. We cannot adequately answer the question, Which vocation shall I choose?
without facing the question behind that: What is
the purpose of life? To the extent that we do not
pursue the most important and basic questions of
all, we are isolated from reality and imprisoned in
immediacies. The results finally become disastrous. We may concentrate only on the data emphasized by the physical sciences and perfect an arse-
nal of nuclear weapons. The outcome may be
oblivion for humanity because we neglected to explore ethical and religious data. One of the noblest
activities of humanity will then produce one of the
most diabolical consequences of history. Without
the warmth of love and the guidance of values
there is no solid basis for adopting priorities for action.

Building conclusions on the whole of reality also
takes us beyond simply sense experiences of the
immediate external environment. We have no
physiological sense organs for directly observing
such realities as magnetism or parts of the spectrum known as "invisible light." Some of our most
important experiences come to us by means that

transcend the senses—like love, or memory, or the sense that we are moving into a future. Henry Moore was after something fundamental when he tried to get into his sculpture a spiritual vitality or power that he saw as more moving than beauty and deeper than the senses. There are facts to which calipers cannot be applied, and truths which cannot be seen through a microscope. If the social sciences and religion merely imitate the methods of the physical sciences, they are likely to attempt a reckless application of quantitative methods to problems to which they are not adapted and to let essential facts slip out without a trace. After their first months in America, the Pilgrims might have looked only at the number of their company who had died and the hardships still ahead. This would have been devastatingly deceptive. Because they saw more than this, instead of returning on the *Mayflower* they held a thanksgiving celebration.

"We are at a moment," wrote Theodore Roszak, "when the reality to which scientists address themselves comes more and more to be recognized as but one segment of a far broader spectrum." [3] Comprehending reality requires openness to human experience in all its depth and complexity. Persons have feelings as well as ideas. As Pascal suggested, there are "reasons of the heart." The social scientist would not get far without taking feelings into account if he wanted to deal with neurotic or delinquent behavior, or motivation in industry, or social change. The central human experiences of selfhood, freedom, or value also go beyond sense experiences. Persons have aesthetic and religious experiences. These need to be rationally interpreted in the light of other data, but nevertheless these experiences are part of the data to be taken into account. These experiences are inaccessible to the positivistic methods of an oversimplified scientism. When tested by more broadly empirical methods, a mystic's awareness of the full range of reality may turn out to be more thoroughly scientific than the work of those scientists who narrow their attention to a limited range of consciousness.

For another thing, truth is to be found not only by detached objectivity but also by involved commitment. Action and reflection both contribute to each other. Things look different from the inside of an organization or after one has adopted a point of view. This may also, of course, become a source of blindness without careful testing to avoid bias. The sociologist finds value in participant observation, but he has also developed safeguards through comprehensive observation. Involvement may lead to bias, but detachment may lead to sterility and neglect of essential data.

Wherever comprehensive views of total reality are important, the scholarly specialization associated with science becomes a danger. With rapidly expanding knowledge, specialization is necessary to research all the details. Yet specialization becomes disastrous if we do not pay attention to those who relate the general conclusions of specialized disciplines in more complete wholes. To see a person as a doctor or dentist sees him, in terms of body temperature or the number of cavi-

ties in his teeth, is not to see the whole person.
Adding a psychologist and a sociologist would
help, but all four together would not show us the
whole person either. Whenever we need to be accurate about the whole person, we need at least
the ethicist and the theologian also. Fractional por-
traits become forms of ignorance. A partial view
may at the same time be entirely true and yet
wholly wrong. In the old fable each of the blind
men described the elephant on the basis of limited
research evidence. The tail felt like a rope, the leg
a tree, and the torso a wall. But the fact remains
that an elephant is not like a rope or a tree or a
wall. We need the report of a better-equipped observer, a sighted person combining fragmentary
viewpoints.

Any insight that begins to correspond to the
vastness of reality must be comprehensive enough
to see the whole as well as the parts, to add integral to analytical thinking. This finally means relating the whole of life to the totality of reality—
which is precisely what religion aims to do. Only
religion uniquely insists upon this completely
comprehensive approach, including as a foundation for both attitude and action all types of experience, past and present, spiritual and secular, immediate and ultimate. Religion works at an
integration of the whole that is consistent with accumulated knowledge in all other fields, and it
adds the most important approach of all, the holistic dimension, without which all other knowledge
is only preparatory. If the scientific approach is to
contribute to deliverance instead of devastation, it

must include the holistic and ultimate dimensions of religion. Instead of religion being outmoded by empirical, scientific enquiry, a thoroughly scientific method demonstrates the need for religion.

Rebellion Against Superstition

To make their unique contribution, the teachings of religion must also pass the empirical test. Superstitions are to be sorted out from authentic traditions. The contents of the Bible, for example, can continue to be honored only if they stand up under inquiry and validation. Simply quoting the Bible proves nothing. Much, though not all of it, resulted from a valid empirical process. Psalmists observed nature and joined this with other religious experiences in their views of God. Out of his personal relationships Hosea came to see new dimensions of love. Jesus was sensitively aware of the lilies in the field, the love of parents toward prodigal sons, and his own religious experience. In evaluating Scriptural material, we need similarly to use the vast accumulation of evidence that is now available to us.

Considerable sections of the Bible do not meet this test. Our knowledge about reality may well lead us to reject those miracles which are contrary to more adequate evidence, or the theory of disease as demon possession, or the virgin birth of Jesus, or the second coming as a physical future event. As Bultmann said, "It is impossible to use electric light and the wireless and to avail ourselves of modern medical and surgical discoveries, and at the same time to believe in the New Testament world of daemons and spirits." To expect persons to believe such archaic doctrine "is to make the Christian faith unintelligible and unacceptable to the modern world." [4]

When aspects of belief deal with comparatively unimportant matters, we can continue to disagree. There is little point in spending time arguing with those who are able to hold minor ancient beliefs together with other seemingly contradictory modern beliefs about reality. There are more important issues to face in the modern world. When, however, outmoded beliefs become obstacles to another person's growth, then more needs to be said. A young American living in India reported: "When the missionaries told me I had to believe in the physical resurrection to be a Christian, that turned me off. It closed the door between me and Christianity. I said, 'Then I can't be a Christian.'" Fortunately she learned that she did not need to believe this particular dogma. At the same time, after rigorous testing she and many others can accept a great long list of Biblical insights, including the way of love, the religious interpretation of life and nature, or the way of Jesus as a life-style.

To fasten on crucial truth and to reject imperfect or outdated notions actually strengthens religious faith. A soundly critical process, instead of being reductionist, is actually expansionist. If Jesus was born through the same sexual process as any man, then his style of life becomes more possible and more compelling for us also. If we do not get hung up on discussions of his physical resurrection, then

we have more time to explore the extremely important spiritual realities that were the heart of the
"resurrection event." If there is consistency in
physical laws, then the universe is more dependable, and we have the possibility of making creative decisions with greater confidence and under
more powerful obligations. If, as Jesus taught, love
rather than vengeance characterizes God, then our
ethical conclusions will be considerably different
and more sound. The more solid the grounding for
beliefs, the more likely is action to be fulfilling and
creative over a wider area of life.

Since ancient days we have learned much
regarding the implementation of Biblical principles. For example, the Biblical way of dealing with
the inequality of rich and poor through personal
charity may now become a support for reaction. We
have discovered better ways than paternalism for
providing equal opportunity and protecting human
dignity, at the same time that we still very much
need the Biblical emphasis on actively and radically meeting the needs of the needy. A dynamic,
ever-living God, or source of truth, still continues
to speak in every new generation. We may have
developed considerably different ways of express-
ing what we mean by God, but we still need the
invitation to deep devotion to the ultimate. We can
now be more precise and illuminating regarding
the detailed meaning of love, but the Biblical principle of transcending selfishness to a higher priority for the neighbor is still indispensable.

New problems have emerged that are not mentioned in the Bible, such as the control of nuclear

energy or the computerization of life. There is no
use pretending that the Bible solves all our specific problems, because it does not. On the other
hand, it is disastrous to contend that we can solve
our problems without the kind of contribution
made by the Bible. We do not need to feel guilty
about not reading the Bible from cover to cover, or
every day. We should still feel very inadequate if
we are not well acquainted with major sections car-
rying fundamental insight.

The Bible has become less popular among many
people because religious leaders have often made
claims for it that could not be substantiated. Then
when their promises were not redeemed the entire
Bible was discarded as worthless. The Bible is too
important to be used inaccurately. The Bible was
never intended to be a book of science or a detailed program for meeting specific problems
through all the centuries. It does provide us with a
basic point of view about ultimate reality and basic
guidelines for moral decision. These contributions
are so fundamental that we cannot afford to have it
rejected. These values to be found in the Bible are
much more likely to be accepted if we separate
them from the dated material which is also to be
found in Scripture. In this respect if some religious
leaders claimed less for the Bible, they could gain
greater influence for it.

If one thinks that truth is best discovered by empirical observation and rational inquiry, how is it
related to the concept of revelation which religion
seems often to have stressed? The answer depends
on one's definition of terms. If a person defines

"hammer" as a screwdriver for sawing wood, he would answer questions about it considerably differently than if he defined a hammer as a tool for pounding nails. If we mean by revelation an overpowering thrust by God into the mind of a person in conflict with the laws of the universe and the evidence of reality, then we would have to say that revelation does not take place. God does not blast thunderbolts from the blue with messages attached. He does not play favorites in dictating documents to mindless men who use merely muscle in the process of recording. Revelation in this sense would make God arbitrary and spasmodic and domineering, instead of consistent, dependably present, and loving.

There are other senses, however, in which revelation is part of the reality we know. Things must be disclosed if they are to be discovered. Pulling up the shade will let no sunshine into the room unless the sun is shining. One can describe this by saying that God always takes the initiative. In this sense, revelation and discovery are two sides of the same coin, and all known truth is revealed truth. In another sense, revelation may be thought of as the novel element in conclusions derived from research. A genius struck on the head by a falling apple adds to his feeling of pain an idea about gravitation. Such clarification or creative insight may emerge gradually, or it may break into the consciousness suddenly during a spell of insomnia in the middle of the night. The moment when truth appears may come unannounced, but it comes best to one who has lived long enough with facts and figures to allow a sudden synthesis. Revelation in this sense comes to minds prepared to receive it. It is the last step in the empirical process.

So long as we remain sensitive to reality and open to the unknown, we can expect breakthroughs into new truth just as amazing in the future as in the past. Laser beams, cybernation, and organ transplants will be made obsolete by even more thrilling discoveries. This will not happen unless we prune away what is false, outdated, and unable to survive critical scrutiny. Sharper methodological tools will make it possible to speak with positive assurance of the essentials of religious faith and to provide a dependable foundation upon which life can confidently be built. With total engagement through our entire beings with all aspects of reality, including the holistic concerns of religion, what might we not accomplish in releasing ultimate resources? There is liberation, meaning, and empowerment in the force of truth. Why should we dilute it with superstition? Why should we be so preoccupied with a part of reality as to perpetuate falsehood about the whole of things?

Churches have often made religious faith incredible and hypocritical. They have stressed the unbelievable or concentrated on ritual unrelated to reality. Consequently, many modern persons have turned away from this caricature of religion in the direction of popular secularism. Yet secularism in turn has also proved so unsatisfying and superficial that there is a continuing longing for superior religious resources. To provide a more satisfying version there are three major questions any adequate religion must answer: What is the central meaning of reality? How can I relate to the most essential power for existence and fulfillment? What is the most important guide for the choices of life? These matters will be dealt with in the next three chapters.

2

BELIEF IN GOD:
UNTHINKABLE OR UNAVOIDABLE?

What is the most important thing going on if we take into account everything that exists? Is there a central meaning to things that can deliver us from uncertainty and deep anxiety to confidence, courage, and satisfying fulfillment? Asking what is the most ultimate or whole leads directly to the question of the nature and existence of God. Is it true that there is a "God-shaped blank" at the center of existence? Or perhaps for most persons the blank is a blur. More numerous than those willing to say "God is dead" are those who drift into a "God is a ghost" position. Comparatively few persons apparently believe that there is nothing that can be called "God." Many more have stripped so much off the concept that only a ghostlike mist seems left.

Modern persons understandably find some concepts of God utterly incredible. They reject as misleading or bizarre a view of God as a meticulous scorekeeper in the sky, hovering in space and assigning lost souls to a fiery hell somewhere in the bowels of the universe. Nor is it true to the best we know, to picture God as an arbitrary dictator or celestial manipulator pushing people around. Certainly God is not the torturer of the condemned, nor is he so intent on punishing wrongdoing that only the death of Jesus can be accepted as a substitute. Nor is God an indulgent parent who rewards the righteous with wealth, turning loyal followers into millionaires. Thoughtful persons reject the very common practice of accepting God as a reinforcer of our national, racial, or class prejudices. God is not a magnified human being remotely residing on the top floor of a three-level universe, with an adversary devil controlling things in the basement. Given prevailing views of the universe, God is not to be separated from the rest of reality. He does not float somewhere in a supernatural realm. Nor is God simply another name for present human ignorance—a "God in the gaps" of human knowledge. The rejection of that kind of God comes easily. If this is what it means to believe in God, then we can anticipate a growing number of atheists. Some ideas about God are so crude or naïve that intelligent persons should reject them. Sensitive persons understandably find such beliefs an obstacle to a religious life. But they do not need to believe these things. For a long time many theists have not believed them either. Such a mis-

shapen God never existed. The disappearance of
such false views is a desirable preparation for
greater clarity about God. As Meister Eckhardt
said, "Only the hand that erases can write the true
thing."

If we are to believe in God today, it is because of
what we find the nature of reality to be. We refer to
God not as a cloak for ignorance but as a consequence of our knowledge. We expect to find God
not on the outer fringes of the universe but in the
midst of our existence. We find intimations of his
presence and activity not in stories about spooks
and goblins but in well-authenticated observations
about the world and people. Modern theologians
who share this approach move also in a long tradition. In the Bible, God was considered not as aloof
from but as very much involved in the creative
movements of nature and history. Luther referred
to finding God behind the "masks" or "veils" of
our environment. Bonhoeffer likewise saw that
"God is the 'beyond' in the midst of our life." [5]
Bultmann maintained that the divine or the transcendent is to be found not by leaving this world
but by remaining in it and allowing available reality to become transparent enough to see our relationship to God.[6] Sociologist Peter Berger sees
"signals of transcendence within the empirically
given human situation." These signals are natural
phenomena that point to a larger or more ultimate
aspect of reality.[7]

To be sure, the whole and the ultimate are
always greater than our views about them. Finite
minds cannot fully know the infinite. Human be-

ings can no more comprehend God completely
than mosquitoes can describe the planets, or
crickets on the wharf can explore the depths of the
sea. Any aspect of reality fully comprehended is no
God. God is not the private property of the suburbanite nor is he the caged possession of any nation.
We cannot put the universe in our pockets, trap
eternity in a box, or compress all meaning into the
human mind. In the dramatic terms of Isa. 55:9,
God must always be pictured as saying, "For as the
heavens are higher than the earth, so are my ways
higher than your ways and my thoughts than your
thoughts." The greatest wisdom of man always
brings us to the edge of mystery. As Roszak expressed it, "Mystery is truth's dancing partner." [8]
Awe and wonder are still appropriate responses
before God.

Since man cannot completely know God, there is
room for a healthy pluralism in religious beliefs, at
the same time that there can be general agreement
on the chief essentials. Churches are full of people
with unorthodox views about God or Jesus. Many
faithful members do not believe all of the Apostles'
Creed or the doctrine of the Trinity or the deity of
Jesus. It comes as a great relief to many to realize
that they do not have to believe these things. Yet
there is abundant evidence for belief in a transcendent aspect of reality which we can call God.

Perhaps this is the place to pause for a brief exer-
cise in definition. Some persons feel uncomfortable about using the word "God" to refer to part or
all of the transcendent dimension of reality. The
word used is not nearly so important as taking

seriously the reality being described. While some may prefer to substitute another phrase, I will continue to use the word "God" both for historic continuity and because the essential connotations are still descriptive for me.

The word "transcendent" carries some repelling connotations. I am using it here not to refer to that which exists apart from material and social reality but to refer to that which is not fully comprehended or actualized by any person or material object, even at its best. The transcendent refers to the whole of things, which is more inclusive than any part. It refers to the ultimate instead of anything more immediate and superficial. It includes the unrealized, which exists as potentiality. The transcendent is not supernatural since it is an aspect of existing or natural reality. It is supernormal in that it thrusts beyond persons, the physical world, and their relationships as they are customarily conceived. The transcendent is an aspect of reality that brings a transforming power or creative thrust within reality.

When the scientific method is applied to the kind of comprehensive data described in the last chapter, scientists may be regarded as allies in the discovery of transcendence. Theologians and scientists can supplement each other in the search for a more adequate view of reality. Startling new discoveries can then be expected in religion as in other areas of knowledge. Far from undermining religious faith, the more that scientists discover about the nature of reality, the more compelling are the reasons for believing in God. Instead of a "death of God" as man comes of age, we might more appropriately speak of a "birth of God."

Many of us remain unaware of this larger dimension of reality because we are occupied only with those things near at hand or most evident. We live in a distorted dream world. The actual universe is much vaster. We repeatedly frustrate the actualization of our potentialities because we do not pay attention to all the data. Our false conclusions then become just as suicidal as though we drove into an intersection having looked only one way and never having seen the truck speeding from the other direction. We scarcely ever see the world of nature or feel its regular rhythms. We no longer wake up to see sunrises, nor do we glimpse the stars through the smog or the city lights. In air-conditioned cocoons and concretized cities we have blocked out the full glory of the seasons. We do not feel intimately placed in a network of natural and human relationships—and as for lengthy pauses to contemplate the ultimate, they are antithetical to typical urban time schedules. No wonder we do not know what the universe—or man, or God—is like.

There are minute crawlers in the earth that find their entire universe bounded by the root system of a single clump of grass. They know nothing of the beauty of billions of dewdrops on spider webs, violins in the silent night, the ecstasies of creative love, or the aspirations built into Gothic cathedrals and modern painting. Human beings have the same problem as the crawlers in the dirt. How often do we simultaneously hold together one grain of sand on a vast desert and unbelievable galaxies in space, each scale on every fish in the depth of the sea and Einstein's theory of relativity, the fury of a bombing attack and a hero liberating a nation or healing a child in the ghetto? One of the greatest dramas in all literature (Job 38:18) has God ask, "Have you comprehended the expanse of the earth?"

One cartoon showed a man and his wife looking at the Grand Canyon. The husband was saying, "Suddenly everything seems so insignificant— with the possible exception of the payments still due on the dishwasher and garbage disposal." Even the Grand Canyon is not a wide enough perspective to put the dishwasher into context. For valid conclusions we need to do our thinking in a still more comprehensive setting. Life disintegrates if all the God we know is superstition, or all the sex we know is lust, or all the virtue we know is selfishness, or all the peace we know is preparation for war. Widely familiar are recent emphases on the intensification of experience, as stressed in the counter-culture or in relationship-training groups. The extensification of experience is at least as important.

When we gain some approximation to a view of the whole, there are several observations about reality that can scarcely be denied and that provide solid grounds for the religious life. Different persons will be impressed by various ones of these observations, as presented in the rest of this chapter. Nevertheless, by pursuing any one of these, or several in combination, one can find a convincing basis for belief in God.

God as Ground of Being

Inquisitive search for the essential nature of things and for the deepest meanings of existence requires a probe toward the ultimate which lies beyond the more immediate. Motion toward the ultimate can be illustrated by the question, What is a chair? Moving through the questions behind the questions, we would have to continue to ask, What is wood . . . and electrons . . . and energy . . . and the interlocking nature of reality? Or we might ask, What should I do this morning? and answer it by deciding to go to work. Then there are still further questions: Why should I work? What is the purpose of life? What sustains that purpose? How is this related to all that exists? Regardless of the interest with which we begin we finally get to questions such as: Who am I? Why am I? What should I become? What is the meaning of it all?

Try holding in awareness every leaf that blows in the forest, every stamen on every tiny flower in the desert, every baby in the villages of the Amazon, all the mice in Manhattan tenements, the frieze of the Parthenon, each screw in an installation of computers, the planets in their courses, and yourself sitting here reading this book. How does one relate the totality of all existence? There is a ground of being more fundamental than the chair on which you are sitting. There are considerations more lasting than the immediacy of life and more decisive than superficial observations.

For one thing, entities that exist do not contain within themselves the supporting power of their own being. For example, human beings are not self-sufficient. We stand on an earth we did not make and use powers we did not generate. We are dependent not only on chemicals and air, but on that on which chemicals and air are dependent. There is, without any reasonable doubt, something beyond nature and ourselves as they most superficially appear simply in physical or psychological terms. There is something more powerful and basic, something that reveals the meaning of existence. This something can be called God. This element in reality Paul Tillich called the ultimate ground of being, or power of being. He spoke of a Being out of which beings come, a fundamental sustaining force, an energizing power that sustains what is.

From this point of view God is not another space-time object, like a galaxy or a grasshopper. Rather, God is thought of as a distinctive aspect, quality, or dimension of the totality of things. God, as Being itself, is the unconditional ground on which all else is dependent. This makes everything else different. God is in all that exists and at the same time transcends all else that exists. God can be thought of as present in persons and in the universe, yet not identical with persons and with the universe. This is somewhat similar to the fact that a person is more than his physical body, and his or her environment is more than the physical

universe. But the spiritual "more" is not separated
from the physical. Rather, it shows itself in it.

We no longer think of a two-story universe with
God on the top floor. We find glory and transcendence in the present world. God does not appear at
particular times and places to manipulate a change
and then withdraw. God is related to the world and
to us, not incidentally or occasionally, but fundamentally and steadily. The common world about
us is continuously infused with holiness or sacred-
ness. The myths of the Hebrews had God say to
Moses, "Take off the shoes from your feet, for the
place where you are standing is holy ground" (Acts
7:33). Tillich put it in these words: "The universe
is God's sanctuary. Every work day is a day of the
Lord, every supper a Lord's supper, every work
the fulfillment of a divine task, every joy a joy in
God." [9] This is akin to the Biblical idea that "he is
not far from each one of us, for 'In him we live and
move and have our being' " (Acts 17:27–28).

One can accept this and also feel a sense of com-
patibility with the modern physicist who no longer
thinks of matter as the ultimate reality. The universe is now regarded as basically a complex com-
pounding of pulses of matter and energy. The most
fundamental realities that we consider material
things are not bits of substance, but relationships,
processes, and events. As one physicist puts it,
matter is "much more like a delicate fabric of dynamic interrelationships than an edifice of hard
building blocks." [10] Astronomy and ecology join
with physics in suggesting that everything is related to everything else, and that a basic common

component is energy. The world is not silent and dead. It is vibrant and living. Man's life interacts with a dynamic world. Martin Buber saw that it was possible to view a tree as an "it," seeing it as wood and leaves, or as an expression of natural laws. But he also saw that we might be so bound up in a relationship to a tree that we valued it for its own sake and listened to its communication to us; then the tree could become a kind of "thou." As we recognize relationships with many things, Buber felt that "in each Thou we address the eternal Thou." [11] We share a primal reality, Being itself, with trees, with an ant crawling over a twig, with the tables at which we sit, and with the totality of the universe. We are part of one vast network of living reality.

Our relationship to the ground of all being is more central than food-getting activities or entertainment, or than the growth of a tree or the movement of a planet—though it is related to all of these. God as ground of being has the first claim to unconditional devotion. This is the ultimate concern of our existence which we take seriously without reservation.

Order as Evidence of God

Another part of the actuality of existence is a significant order and dependability. Reality as we experience it is not an erratic jumble of disconnected phenomena. There are sequences and regularities in nature and in human beings. With all the microcosms within microcosms, and all the macrocosms beyond macrocosms, there is unity in diversity. Things are held together in a network of relationships and interdependency, and also in continuity through time. We can correctly speak of a universe and of a history. This is a matter of scientific observation as well as of religious experience.

Nature shows innovative spontaneity, as does man. There is an aspect of indeterminacy among small particles, and the "laws of nature" are probability laws. Yet dynamic action occurs within a framework of dependable continuity. Although cats change as they grow, they remain cats. They do not change into sharks or artichokes. Planets move but do not collide. Under the right conditions coal is formed. The surgeon can depend upon certain limiting consequences if he removes an organ. After traveling to the moon, astronauts can land within a mile of the recovery ship. Industry can manufacture identical parts to fine tolerances. Even while other forces also operate, love still remains powerful. We do not gather grapes from thistles, nor prolong the lives of citizens by exploding nuclear bombs over their cities. Within a complex interrelationship of influences, every movement for social reform assumes orderly patterns by which its program can lead to human improvement. Roger Garaudy has observed, "The philosophy of the absurd is neither for the learned man nor for the revolutionary." [12]

Accurately to see the whole of things is also to see that there is that which holds reality together in unity and order. This too we can call God. In this sense we can agree with Walt Whitman that "a mouse is miracle enough to stagger sextillions of infidels." In magnitudes and intricacies considerably beyond a mouse, scientific inquiry reveals a reality that hangs together. Science itself is possible only because of a faith in pattern and meaning behind the miscellaneous and the seemingly contradictory manifestations of reality. Under every scholarly discipline lies a belief in coherence and intelligibility.

Another way of approaching this is to ask whether this kind of universe is best explained as due to accident or design. In our common experience we know nothing about the process by which this kind of universe could be possible by chance conditions and endlessly repeated fortuitous events. To think so requires superstitious, blind credulity utterly foreign to our empirical observation of how such things occur. Development and orderly design are not produced simply by many independent elements in inert existence without some greater power to relate them and hold them together in a living whole. Grains of sand in a high desert wind do not happen to strike each other in such a way as to produce an irrigation project. Children do not learn calculus without a network of intentional human support. When one discovers an orderly universe evolving toward greater richness of fulfillment, the most reliable hypothesis is that there is a basic capability for design and a consistent, creative power at work. Whether this can be thought of as a personal designer will be discussed in a later section. But at least we need to recognize that there is an aspect of reality which

introduces an orderly force transcendent to the less
ultimate aspects of existence. This can be appropriately thought of as God.

Suffering as Denial of God

There is, however, a strong argument on the
other side of the case. This is an orderly universe,
but there are also eruptions of apparent chaos and
disorder. There is randomness, wastefulness, and
brutality in natural evolutionary processes. There
is creative movement, but it may be blocked.
There is the emergence of values, but also of evil.
The processes of the universe not only build but
also destroy. The reality of suffering, whether from
natural evil or human choice, makes it hard to say
that there is a good God at the center of things,
especially if he is thought of as an all-powerful
God.

Are these negative factors at all consistent with
the picture of a dynamic and orderly universe?
Surprisingly, they may turn out to be part of a consistent pattern. For one thing, suffering and difficulty can themselves be seen as instrumental values. In our experience there is no personal growth
or social improvement without the pain of facing
resistance to change. Muscles are developed not
by sunbathing on the beach but by sawing wood.
The potentialities of the human mind are realized
not by looking up answers in the back of the book
but by solving difficult problems. Likewise, social
and spiritual growth accompany the struggle
against imperfection or evil. If it is creatively met,

suffering can have educational value. Natural evil
resulting from a growing and incomplete universe
may well have a similar important purpose in the
nature of things.

Sigmund Freud was once told the story of a
surgeon who complained that if he ever reached
the eternal throne, he would bring a cancerous
bone and ask God what he had to say about it.
Freud is reported to have replied that if he found
himself in a similar situation, his chief reproach to
the Almighty would be for not giving him a better
brain to deal with disease. Difficulties and suffering can activate within persons powers that were
previously dormant. Toynbee and others have also
pointed out the dangers to society when it becomes content with enjoying values achieved in
the past rather than responding creatively and
painfully to new problems. Affluence and ease
tend to stifle creativity and to contribute to the collapse of culture.[13]

If the person who suffers does not grow, others
may be the beneficiaries. Those who die from in-
curable disease or traffic accidents stimulate the
application of energy toward the discovery of new
cures or preventive techniques. Or individual suffering may contribute to a more widespread release of hidden resources in the human spirit.
George Jordan, a young minister dying of cancer,
said to his wife: "Evonne, we have a ministry here.
We have to show people how to die." Those who
suffer vicariously in this way may thereby realize
the central purpose of life. Theirs can be the self-
realization that comes from sacrificial service to

others in love. The literary beauty of the fifty-third chapter of Isaiah is matched by its writer's profound insight when he observes "with his stripes we are healed" (Isa. 53:5).

To put it in another way, there are four values that most of us want very much. It is hard to see how we could have them without suffering. One of these is dynamic growth. We do want the exhilaration of personal development in an infinitely developing universe. We would not want to be permanent babies perpetually living in a playpen with food, music, and toys piped in. This would become an eternity of bland banality and boredom. That the world is not made this way is a tribute to an imaginative and benevolent God. The only trouble with the traditional concept of angels is that there is no place for them to go and nothing to do. They are already there. If there is to be growth, there must be immaturity and imperfection. If there is to be a possibility of dynamic achievement in curing disease, there must be disease to cure.

A second widespread desire is for human freedom. Yet freedom inevitably carries with it the possibility of wrong choice. Social evil is the consequence not of God's specific initiative but of humanity's choices. If God willed the carnages in Auschwitz, Hiroshima, Biafra, or East Pakistan, he is a monster. But he did not will them. God allows them to happen as a necessary consequence of freedom. But these are the evils which people perpetrate. As a third desired value, we would prefer to live in a dependable world in which appropriate consequences reliably follow action. The good life would be impossible if we could not choose with this kind of assurance. Yet this inevitably means also that suffering follows humanity's evildoing. In addition to dynamic growth, freedom, and dependability we also treasure a fourth value, interaction among persons. Human relationships are one of the greatest gifts life brings. If we want to be the beneficiaries of the good that others do, then by the same relationship we are also affected by the evil that others do.

If everything were continuously perfect without hardship, the situation would also be static without significant freedom of choice leading to dependable consequences in interaction among persons. This is recognized by the parent who, because he loves his children, makes sure that they face problems. Too great indulgence or sheltering leads to deterioration. Nothing but peace and quiet may be fine for a vacation, but not for daily living. Suffering and difficulty can be seen as a part of God's good universe. Both the Old and the New Testament carry the suggestion that God allows those whom he loves to suffer. (Prov. 3:12; Heb. 12:6.) There is a rabbinic saying, "The man who went forty days without trouble was past hope, since this was a sure sign that God had given him up in despair." This is not a complete solution to the problem of suffering. There is still much to be known about baffling events in life. But this does suggest a way of approaching the problem which relates it to the roots of goodness and order in the world.

In addition to natural evil and the capacity of man to do evil (traditionally called "original sin"), there is also natural and original goodness. Reality does support the development and enhancement of human life. Seeds do sprout, the body does have a tendency to heal, the mind and personality have amazing capacity for growth. Just as suffering and evil constitute problems for the theist, so goodness and dynamic potentiality constitute problems for the atheist. In ways suggested above, it is easier to explain suffering and imperfection or incompleteness on a theistic basis than it is to explain goodness and growth on a naturalistic basis or on the basis of a malevolent God.

Furthermore, the events of our years are not so great a tragedy if we see spiritual development as the highest value to be enjoyed. Spiritual growth is always possible even during disaster. It may even be aided by physical and social difficulties. It is also more realistic to see a human lifetime as part of an eternal process. It is not necessary to believe in eternal personal life to accept what has been said about suffering. But those who, even in terms not completely understood, have a sense of living relationships continuing beyond what we call death can see human suffering in a different light. Yet even without believing in life after death, it is still possible to recognize that it is through continuous appearance of new problems and creative struggle to solve them that the highest and most enduring values are realized.

In a developing universe always incomplete, God himself is continuously and creatively active against evil and suffering. This is consistent with any of the views of God suggested in this chapter.

There is in all of them a dynamic element. God is at work in a world that is changing and unfinished. Instead of the universe being a static entity, created complete in seven days, the process of creation continues. When the theory of evolution was first accepted, Biblical interpreters stretched the original seven days of Genesis into aeons, but saw them all as behind us. Now we see ourselves as somewhere in the middle or even near the beginning of the "days" of creation.

One of the deep insights of the Bible is that God himself suffers. The crucifixion of Jesus is one dramatic way of showing this. Men saw the spirit of God in Jesus, at work in a hostile world, and suffering the consequences. Jesus identified himself with the poor and the needy, attacked dehumanizing customs, and paid the penalty for revolutionary demands against entrenched power structures. God can be viewed as continuing the same activity.

Where two or three people are gathered genuinely loving each other, God is there supporting and intensifying. Where two or three are present needlessly dropping a bomb from a plane, God is there too, suffering, condemning the act, seeking to awaken opposition to the monstrosity. The power of God is also shared with persons who respond. We too change the world situation. What God can do is affected by each of our acts, since God always works within the world as it is at any moment. What can be done depends to a considerable extent on our willingness to cooperate. There are tremendous potentialities for good or for evil in the

world. It is part of man's destiny to determine
which he will enhance and which he will oppose.
In the full panorama of existence, life is not absurd. Reality is not meaninglessness. It has direction. Life can be purposive. We can cooperate with
God as the dynamic element in reality, struggling
always to enhance the good.

The Reality of Potentiality

Unquestionably there exist unrealized possibilities in persons, nature, and society. The physical
and social sciences unite to emphasize the lavish
abundance of potentialities in both the expanding
universe and in humankind. There seems to be an
infinity of amazing outcomes still to be realized—
in personal intimacy, social justice, equal opportunity, love, the destruction of all dehumanizing
structures, the full liberation of humanity. No matter how far we have developed, there are always
new attainments still to be achieved and enjoyed.
Beyond limits ordinarily accepted ours can be an
unprecedented future. A religious way of express-
ing this psychological reality is to say that we
have the possibility of becoming children of God.
(John 1:12; Rom. 8:14–19; Eph. 1:5.) Every moment we stand in a position similar to the man and
the woman who are just being married, or the new-
born baby first being laid in a crib. Who can say
what lies ahead? There was a power that was in
Jesus, that has been manifested through the centuries in giants of the human spirit, and that now is
latent within us also. These potentialities exist as

an aspect of reality. They transcend all that has been substantively actualized up to this point. The sum total of these transcendent possibilities can be called God. Or we may speak of God as the power that established and sustains these possibilities, and that therefore is present in every imperfect situation as an impulse toward improvement.

This introduces hope into the human situation, in contrast with deeply rooted existential despair. Peter Berger sees human hope as one of the "signals of transcendence" in our common experience.[14] The potentialities of reality provide a basis for such hope. With spontaneity and joy we can celebrate God as the source and ground for hope as well as for life. Some religious movements have seen signs of the coming of Christ in situations that were getting worse. Even today some people are convinced that when the situation gets bad enough, there will be a second coming and Christ will set all things right. The religion of the future is more likely to see signs of the action of God at those times when things are getting better. Or, it might be said that God confronts man not only at his weakest point (sin) but even more at his strongest point (potentiality).

Potentialities can be described in terms of values or desirable qualities. Persons may incorporate more of beauty, goodness, and love. Society may embody more of justice and freedom. Some people prefer to think of God as the sum total of values in all that exists. Gandhi's thought included a concept of God as truth. One of the Biblical themes is, "God is love, and he who abides in love abides in

God" (I John 4:16). Muriel Lester expanded this in her early-morning prayer, "Thou art shining beauty, radiant joy, creative power, all-pervading love, perfect understanding, purity and peace."

Other persons prefer not to think of God as synonymous with values, but rather as the source and sustainer of values. There is something in reality that is hospitable or supportive of values. There is that which tends to nurture and sustain all created good. This is the kind of world in which love, for example, is both a possibility and a necessity. Love has a cosmic ground. We may say that God embodies love and beauty and wisdom, and that he is also active in enhancing such values in the world.

Even though we recognize it in only a very elementary or fleeting way, all of us have hidden away some sense of moral obligation. Every twinge of what we commonly call "conscience" is a reminder that values are a transcendent aspect of our existence, and that we harbor some sense of unrealized possibility. We find in reality itself these internalized generalizations which become guides to conduct. Experiences of life and history confirm the desirability of integrity, justice, love. We identify the good or the right because they are written in the structures of existence. There are dependable consequences for action. Ignorance and exploitation lead to the disintegration and destruction of social values. In the long run and from the total point of view, moving toward not-yet-realized values such as mutual concern and cooperation contributes to the most complete personal and social enhancement. If we are going to be realistic and hardheaded, we will build on that evidence and accept that fact. That is the way the universe is put together. Any well-lived life includes long concentration on this aspect of the "beyond" in our midst.

God as Creative Process

Not only are potentialities sustained as a part of reality, as suggested above. There is also the power to realize what might be—a drive toward the actualization of potentiality. There is something in the nature of things which makes improvements possible. This is not to suggest inevitable progress but only possible progress. The universe exhibits creativity. God can be thought of as the power to change, or the process of creative becoming that makes for the growth of good. The fundamental force sustaining being and order is also dynamic and directional. Persons and natural processes embody a pull toward the future. Along with continuity there is an impulse to innovate.

Henry Nelson Wieman thought of God as that creative process of interaction among persons which he called "the source of human good." [15] Teilhard de Chardin also saw God in a broader though similar evolutionary aspect of reality. As creation "continues still more magnificently," he felt that the divine "thoroughly permeates all our creaturely energies." [16] John Cobb, building on Alfred North Whitehead, speaks of God as "the call forward," a distinctive element in experience and a push toward creativity beyond our present selves

and the existing world of nature.[17] E. Schillebeeckx proposes that we shift our concepts from
God as the "wholly Other" to God as the "wholly
New." [18] Harvey Cox suggests that God is not so
much "above" the affairs of men as he is
"ahead." [19]

There is something in universal reality that
allows growth or purposive transformation. From
the formation of our present universe, through the
appearance of simple forms of life on this earth, to
the development of man and civilization, to whatever surprises the future certainly holds, a creative
process is quite apparent. Empirical studies have
concluded that, in spite of temporary eddies, over
the very long run there has been an evolutionary
movement in both physical reality and human development from simple to more complex structures
and relationships, from qualitative limitation to
qualitative richness and variety, from the inert to
the more dynamic, from comparative insensitivity
to higher capacities for responsiveness, and from
comparative isolation to a more social existence.
There has been an emergence of life, of mind, and
of spirit. Now we may be trembling at the edge of
such a transformation of persons as to make present
humanity the missing link between the apes and
the being that is yet to be.

Science now sees reality as in constant flux. To
accord with reality, a person's style of life must
also be dynamic and growing. This being a world
in process, only creators can thrive in it. No society
endures unless it continuously alters its customs to
adapt to changing conditions. There is without a

doubt that aspect of reality which stimulates the
vision of the artist and of the reformer, the best
research of the scientist and of the technological
engineer, the aspirations of the mystic and of the
saint.

When we recognize the dynamics of creative
change, we are accepting one form of transcendence.
We are affirming processes which we did not es-
tablish and possibilities beyond any existing actualization in man, nature, and their relationships.
Such transcendence is an indisputable aspect of reality. Even if one holds only to the minimal view
of God thus far suggested (as ground of being,
unrealized value, or creative process), one must
conclude that God is continuously active in the
universe. God is not dead, nor is he unemployed,
nor has he emigrated from creation. Nor does God
act only in occasional mighty and miraculous manifestations. God is at work now—here, everywhere,
and always.

Even though we try, we can never remove ourselves from God's presence. We can refuse to cooperate and thereby become a backward drag on the
creative process. Even so, the call to realize potentiality is still there. We could at any moment positively experience God as the power making for liberation, reconciliation, and love. God is at least
somewhat acknowledged by us whenever we are
creatively dissatisfied, or become more alive, or
express caring, or do the right thing, or work for
social reform. Wherever human needs are being
met, wherever exploitation and tyranny are being
opposed, wherever persons discover each other as

brothers and sisters, wherever love challenges injustice, there God is at work. In the picture language of the book of Revelation, God is always saying, "Behold, I make all things new" (Rev. 21:5).

Major Consequences of a
Minimal View of God

Thus far the discussion in this chapter has been about a minimal view of God, outlining the limited list of observations that seem unavoidable on the basis of empirical evidence and which may be widely meaningful for persons of the future. The next section will go into the question of how much more can be believed. But even these minimal unassailable observations allow us reliably to know enough to build life on our insights. Modern persons can affirm with confidence a belief in God. We do not need to say "maybe" or "perhaps" about this any more than about other widely accepted beliefs that we act upon with assurance—like general national priorities or the values of democracy. There are major dimensions of the whole of things, such as a ground of being, orderly relationships, unrealized potentialities, a source of power, creative process. All these exist within reality and permeate all that exists. Yet they are transcendent, in the sense of that which is unfulfilled or beyond our habitual awareness and concern, or on which we are dependent. Taken together, these elements constitute a richly meaningful description of what may well be called God.

This ground for belief in God grows out of our

knowledge rather than out of our ignorance. Many past views of God were explanations of our ignorance, leaving God a hesitant question mark rather than a confident exclamation point. Beyond reasonable doubt for most persons, there is such a transcendent dimension of reality as I have been describing. Denial of the existence of God takes more blind faith, running contrary to the evidence, than does belief in God. As John Macquarrie has written, "The very fact that there is a world rather than just nothing, that this is an ordered and structured world rather than just chaos, and that this world has brought forth spiritual and personal beings, makes atheism a most improbable thesis." [20]

Even such a minimal view of God as has thus far been discussed makes a very great deal of difference in life. For one thing, by inviting attention to the whole and the ultimate it provides a more comprehensive view of reality. This equips us with a more adequate range of knowledge. To ignore the transcendent dimension is to perpetuate comparative ignorance and mediocrity. Disastrous consequences follow action informed by only part of the data. We will keep on fighting wars until we take into account more than appears in the "in" and "out" boxes on the desks of Government officials.

By pushing out the walls of our awareness, a view of God liberates narrow and incomplete lives. We find a source of assurance and hope in the dependability and the dynamic order of things. Resources of power become available from beyond the material and the present. Personal adequacy can be more fully released when life is unified around a single central focus. Little unification of meaning is possible without reference to a more ultimate reality beyond the fragments of existence. Any God a little higher than television and a little lower than sex doesn't unify much of life. By relating it to what is more ultimately important, life is rescued from pointlessness and given significance.

A view of God that helps make sense of our existence also provides important guideposts for conduct. In larger perspective we respond less easily to mere impulse and desire. Awareness of our full environment makes a difference, just as foreign policy is considerably changed when we begin thinking not only of the interest of Americans but also of Iranians. Involvement in improvement becomes a more demanding priority. A life saturated in ultimacy can be better motivated for a heroic, prophetic thrust beyond existing social arrangements. We act against poverty, for example, not only because it is messy regarding human life but because it is rebellion against the central developmental thrust of the universe.

Even a minimal view of God is an important antidote to pride and conformity. Potentiality always constitutes a judgment on actuality. In the light of the transcendent no individual person and no social system is as good as it ought to be. (Those who are self-satisfied or politically conservative, read that sentence again.) Worship becomes a more normal item on a personal agenda, in the sense of modestly attributing worth. The universe is seen to include the worthful. The creative process has

awe-inspiring grandeur. Personal devotions as
meditation become an important part of life. Ultimate meanings cannot be related to complicated
life problems without spending time thinking
about the connection. Prayer in its full meaning is
probably not possible to many persons on the basis
of a minimal view of God. Prayer in a limited sense
might be practiced as an expression of our feelings
and hopes and commitments, largely directed to
ourselves. Prayer in its distinctive meaning would
seem to require recognition of a personal element
in God, a possibility still to be discussed in the
next section of this chapter.

It is not only that modern persons find religious
beliefs incredible. They reject or neglect religion
also because they find it irrelevant or unnecessary.
They do not see that it makes any difference. The
combination of consequences just described adds
up to a crucial difference. It is the difference between two distinctive life-styles. The religious person faces a wider range of questions with more adequate knowledge, surer direction, stronger
motivational support, and greater serenity of meaning. Some may choose not to use the word "God,"
but if one rejects the reality to which the word
refers, life becomes impoverished. If we lose our
capacity for transcendence, in the long run life may
become impossible, because of reduced creativity
in meeting basic threats to society. The distinctive
contribution of religion is that it relates the whole
of life to the whole of reality. All of life consequently is lived on a higher level, within the
context of the transcendent.

A More Maximal Faith: God as Suprapersonal

What pronoun is most suitably used to refer to God? Is it "he/she" or "it"? Those who take what I have referred to as a minimal view of God may prefer the impersonal "it." On this basis they can still have a very serious and significant belief in God, with all the important consequences just listed. Those who see adequate support for a view of God as personal are not content with such a minimal view, however. They regard the consequences of such a limited view as unnecessarily meager.

When we begin to list characteristics of the ultimate or transcendent, in combination they turn out to be closer to the category of the personal than to any other category we know. For one thing, God as minimally described is characterized by dynamic unity in complex diversity. The divine dimension of reality is the element that holds all things together in a basically orderly universe. At the same time God exhibits power in creativity. The power of being in all that exists is an initiating force or process. God acts—with vitality, pulsating energy, aliveness. God is future-oriented, sustaining long-term trends moving in particular directions. Such goal-oriented change is spontaneity with purpose. God is value-regarding, or righteous. Out of the creative process emerge larger possibilities for self-actualization. God manifests justice in the sense of maintaining a long-term structure of consequence. God is not capricious, erratic, altering his creation every morning according to the

passing whim of the day. God is reliable and can
be trusted. God can be characterized as knowledgeable, wise, or intelligent. God has the ability
to comprehend all that in any way touches an extremely complex relationship, the ability to plan a
process for millennia, the ability to cope creatively.
This suggests a cosmic supramind with qualities
such as intelligence and initiative. In addition,
there are qualities in God best designated as benevolent. God is friendly to fulfillment, with the
long trends of evolution moving toward a richer,
more meaningful existence. In spite of suffering,
life as given to us is a prized gift, to be amazingly
and joyously celebrated. Creation exhibits a gener-
ous redundancy of opportunities for development
far beyond what we deserve. There might have
been a malevolent power at the center of the universe. Instead, God enables, supports, and wills
the good for us—which is a definition of wise and
active love.

Add all these up and the sum comes closer to
spirit or personality than to any other available category. These are the kinds of characteristics that
our observation and experience have led us to as-
sociate with personality. The personal is the only
category we have experienced that unites such a
combination of characteristics. We begin to find it
more suitable to use personal pronouns to refer to
God. It becomes easier to see God as an experiencing subject, a self-conscious awareness, a source of
innovative action.

The hypothesis of a personal God has also been
confirmed for many by religious experience. When

other data seemed to point toward such a God, many have tried out the hypothesis and found it confirmed by such experimentation. The possibility of such experiences will be discussed at greater length in the next chapter. The discussion of this matter will not be complete until that section has been read. Here let it simply be said that again and again those who had what they were convinced was an experiential relationship with God have felt that the interaction was not with a system of ideas nor with abstract being or process or value. In mystical experience only the language of interpersonal relationship between God and a human being is found to be adequate or accurate. This concept comes closest to what those experiencing God are trying to report.

In addition to this, it can be argued that personality is the highest category of reality we have found. God as the ultimate in reality must incorporate at least the highest that we know. As Tillich put it, "Man cannot be ultimately concerned about something which is less than he is, something impersonal." [21] Persons have a value and a potentiality that the material world lacks. God must also exhibit such values. To think of God as personal may be inadequate, but to think of God as a thing or a process or a force is even more inadequate.

Some persons prefer the word "spirit" to describe this personal quality. When someone has lost interest or zest or the will to live, we say that he or she is dispirited. The body may still be healthy and the mind may be working brilliantly, but something is missing. Persons such as Lincoln,

Einstein, and Martin Luther King had this quality
added to their physical and mental endowments in
a remarkable way. Something akin to this drive
toward inclusive fulfillment is a characteristic of
the ultimate quality of reality. There is a transcendent creativity, a constructive, energizing, unifying
element in all that exists—the power of spirit
within reality. The machine is not a good model for
describing the universe. An organismic model
seems better suited to a situation in which there
seems to be "an ultimate spontaneity at the base of
things." [22]

As the minds of persons affect the physical, so
we can think of the basic energy of the universe,
which we call God, as affecting all there is. God's
relationship to the rest of the world is more like
the impingement of a person than like the mecha-
nistic impingement of a thing. Leroy Howe
suggests, "It is like the nurture of a parent, and
perhaps even of a friend, rather than like the colli-
sion of one billiard ball with another." [23] God can
have a relationship with us comparable to that
which one human being can have with another. As
John A. T. Robinson put it in *Honest to God*, "To
say that 'God is personal' is to say that 'reality at its
very deepest level is personal,' that personality is
of *ultimate* significance in the constitution of the
universe, that in personal relationships we touch
the final meaning of existence as nowhere else." [24]
While he greatly altered the traditional picture of
God, Tillich also saw the importance of the personal element in an adequate representation. He
wrote, "The symbol of the Personal God is indis-

pensable for living religion." [25]

This is still an empirically based conclusion. Such an explanation is necessary to give coherence to what we observe in reality. The hypothesis is further tested and substantiated in religious experience. This view gives the most meaning and unity to the relevant data in its full and ultimate range. It is based on exploration that is more exhaustive and more sensitive to the depths of life. When Jesus called God "Father" (aside from the masculine connotations in our language) he was stating profound truth.

Of course we must beware of becoming anthropomorphic and making God in our own image. God is of a different order than all particular beings. God is greater than *anything* we can put into words. Reality is shot through with glory and mystery. Describing God in any human category is like trying to sweep back the sea with a broom or to imprison the sun in a matchbox. When we speak of the attributes or characteristics of God, the words we use must be considered as symbols or pointers even more than words usually are. God is not a person in the limited sense that a human being is. The nature of God incorporates the values of personality as we know them. But God is also *very much more*. God is not less personal than human beings are, but more personal. God is not subpersonal, or merely personal, but suprapersonal. God may well transcend the qualities of personality as much as these transcend the physical and material.

The preceding section of this chapter described possible consequences of a minimal view of God.

If we accept God as personal, we can experience
all those consequences and more besides. The possibility of an interpersonal relationship introduces
greater warmth in a more intimate fellowship. If
we think of the most intimate relationship we
know (as perhaps in the family), and then transfer
that to the ultimate center of power and meaning
(far beyond the President of the United States or
the Secretary-General of the United Nations), and
then multiply this intimacy with the ultimate by a
multiplier larger than we can imagine—then we
begin to see the possible relationship that God
offers to us. The personal dimension in God also
makes possible a fuller interaction. Meditation in
personal devotion is possible even with a minimal
view of God. With a maximal view the full range of
prayer becomes easier. It seems right to share our
feelings and longings in genuine conversation.
God is seen as a companion who stands close by,
and who is interested in each of us personally. We
can regard God not only with awe, gratitude, and
admiration but also with affection. Creative power
has become caring presence. The ultimate is also
intimate. In Buber's terms, instead of an "I-it" contact, this becomes an "I-Thou" relationship of love.

All this adds extra excitement to life. The possibilities are even better than we had otherwise suspected. Here are firmer grounds for assurance and
hope, enabling support, sense of direction, motivation, and power. In moving beyond a minimal view
of God we can move into a supraintimate relationship with the suprapersonal God. Far from

being reductionist, a more credible view of God is expansionist. God then penetrates the whole of existence. We no longer need believe in an anthropomorphic God or a separated God or a miracle-working, lawbreaking God. We can believe in God as an aspect of all reality, as everywhere creatively present. Greater consequences for personal living flow from a solid religion of reality than from a shaky structure of superstition.

We cannot escape God, whether we take a minimal or a maximal view. God is here. We meet God in the common life—in our bodies or our work, in music, nature, human aspirations, or religious experiences. We cannot change reality. We can only choose to accept or reject a vital relationship.

It is no good merely to analyze the arguments or to give only intellectual assent. The appropriate response goes far beyond telling a Gallup Poll interviewer that we believe in God. We need also to change our ways of life. The reality of God calls for an either-or type of decision. Do I supremely desire ultimate and transcendent possibilities in God, or do I give priority to the worldly affluence promoted in mass media commercials? What in life is tremendous and what is trivial? In their basic orientation, crowds of theoretical theists these days are really practicing atheists. They make minor modifications in life-style because of ultimate dimensions represented by God. But most of their decisions are still made in loyalty to community customs. They actually worship a variety of contradictory little godlets that parade along the type on newspapers, peek out from behind coffee cups, and in mass rallies jump around on television screens.

The identification of ultimate loyalty is the single most important decision in life. The New Testament speaks of this as a drastic choice, comparable to putting one's hand to the plow and not looking back, or leaving the dead to bury their dead, or taking up one's cross, or selling everything for the pearl of great price. Only such a decisive affirmation allows the emergence of a new being, fantastically liberated and fulfilled.

3

THE ECSTASY OF NEW EXPERIENCE

Who am I if I am properly introduced to myself? What does it mean to be human? Is the authentic person a "little less than God," as the Eighth Psalm puts it, or a little higher than the anthropoid apes, as evolutionary secularists sometimes suggest? Current emphases on human potentialities would seem to place us somewhat closer to the angels and somewhat farther from the apes than traditional religion would seem to suggest. Is this an accurate estimate?

The possibilities for human development are in many ways greater than ever before. We have always expected babies to grow into children and then into adults. What once was considered adulthood is now seen as preliminary to a further maturing of hitherto unrealized possibilities. To support such a succession of surprises there is much more knowledge available than ever before, more understanding of the emotional life and of the possible power in group relationship. Growth groups, alpha waves, superior health care, capacities for friendship, greater leisure, new forms of worship are samples of improved resources. In some respects what was considered mature in the past may now be regarded more nearly as infantile or, at best, adolescent. We can now provide environments for nurturing a new human consciousness. Tagore said, "Every child born into the world brings a message from God, that he is not yet discouraged with man." We can add that every adult in his continued capacity for growth carries the message that God is not yet satisfied with man. True maturity is never a static state. Every life has its greatest climaxes yet to come. As Georgia Harkness once wrote, "He who would say, 'I have arrived,' would thereby confess that he had not yet started." [26]

This capacity for starting that never stops is produced and sustained by the creative processes of the universe. We cannot do this alone. The ultimate initiative is always God's. But this prior initiative has already been taken. God is more eager to give than we are to receive. This is like a safe-deposit box with two keys. God has already inserted and turned his. Man now only needs to turn his key to gain whatever treasures lie behind the door.

The Liberation of Potentiality

Recent world history has pulled the rug out from under any inflated optimism concerning humanity. Our capacities for evil are great enough to allow wars with unprecedented proliferation and sophistication of weaponry. Economic exploitation continues to widen the gap between the rich and the poor nations. Ruthless totalitarianism has appeared in even the most politically mature countries. Hiroshima, My Lai, Belsen, Watergate, and brutality on the streets of every city suggest something lower than the apes rather than anything approaching an angelic status for human beings. Depth psychology has dredged up messy, irrational elements in human conduct. Drug addicts sell their own living necessities or rob others to buy drugs. Sex addicts give up possibilities for full intimacy and social creativity in their preoccupation with quantity and varieties of sex. There are strong tendencies in each of us to grab power over others, to warp the truth to favor our side of the argument, or to rationalize our holding on to more privileges than justice allows. We practice piracy on the resources of the earth, taking for ourselves what belongs to future generations. We repeatedly become accomplices in manslaughter. If shutting a child up in a room and starving it to death is morally a form of murder, then our negligence and exploitation of the Third World implicates us in killing.

A distinguished group of theologians, speaking of the discovery of atomic energy, suggested that man's "proudest powers have always been his

most dangerous sources of peril." [27] Reinhold Niebuhr said of the human spirit, "In its yearning toward the infinite lies the source of both human
creativity and human sin." [28] A remarkable Bible
passage (Rom. 7:15–24) appropriately asks, "Who
will deliver me from this body of death?" Humankind may prove to be the most lethal part of the
universe. Science may become the slave of
ruthless group interests. Churches may become
allies of an unjust *status quo*. The Biblical word is
true: "All have sinned and fall short of the glory of
God" (Rom. 3:23).

At the same time, the doctrine of original sin as
elaborated by some traditional theologians must be
firmly rejected, insofar as it speaks of inherited
guilt or bias toward evil. A just God does not morally condemn us for what our ancestors did. There
is no inevitable warping of life with a bias toward
evil. The possibility of evil is ineradicable but so is
the potentiality for good. We should cosponsor
John Macquarrie's statement, "Some Christian
theologians (myself included) have held that any
doctrine of original sin needs to be counter-
balanced by a doctrine of original righteousness." [29] The doctrine of original sin in its extreme
form has been unpopular among theologians for
some time, though the word concerning this rejection has not always gotten out to the critics of the
church. Yet such a great emphasis on sin and guilt
has continued in many religious groups that a different balance is still called for, with greater emphasis on the potentiality in persons for positive
growth in good. The moral nature of human beings

is ambivalent. Like the amphibious creatures that can live on land or in water, persons may move toward either sainthood or devilry. There is a Hasidic saying: "Everyone must have two pockets, so that he can reach into the one or the other, according to his needs. In his right pocket are to be the words: 'For my sake the world was created,' and in his left: 'I am dust and ashes.' "

Psychological research substantiates this view of the human condition. Research has uncovered much of the murky muck in the unconscious depths of man's perversity, and has revealed the mechanisms by which even our noblest aspirations are thwarted by egoistic motivations. At the same time clinical psychologists recognize the dangers in too great pessimism. A major difficulty among maladjusted and troubled people is that they despise themselves as being worthless and unlovable. Churches sometimes encourage neurotic guilt and self-doubt, when persons would better respond to an emphasis on high self-esteem and greater hope. Churches at their best have seen that we push toward personal health and social improvement more surely when we see ourselves responding to the love of God as persons of worth and potentiality.

Psychological science increasingly reveals the strength of human potentialities for love and creative action. It is estimated that the typical person uses only about 6 to 10 percent of his or her constructive capacities. We have vast physical reserves that we never tap. The human sense of smell or sight could become much more acute than our

training has allowed. Many retired persons discover latent capacities for art or other forms of creativity which they had blocked throughout life.
Brain research suggests that the creative capacity
of the human mind may be, for all practical purposes, infinite. There are dimensions of human capacity in the spiritual realm of which we are just
beginning to become aware (as in extrasensory perception or spiritual healing) and undoubtedly
others of which we are still entirely ignorant. Humanity has a capacity for self-transcendence, the
ability to criticize and improve its conduct and to
turn its potentialities into actualities.

The social sciences demonstrate that group
progress is neither inevitable nor impossible. The
future may hold ever more destructive wars, cruel
totalitarianisms, the rape of the environment,
worldwide conglomerates for human exploitation,
or the extinction of man from the earth. The future
may also bring the conquest of war and poverty, a
superindustrial civilization recovering values of intimacy, and a flowering of the arts, morality, and
religion. Coping with such increasingly complex
social options requires more human resources than
ever before. This is what makes a fuller release of
human potentiality so important, and current efforts to dull sensibilities so devastating. Greater
adequacy depends upon increasing personality resources rather than reducing them through escape
mechanisms, such as drug abuse or even excessive
television viewing. Allowing persons to die without developing their full potentialities is at least as
bad as our current waste of natural resources. This

is a "brain drain" or a "skill spill" which applies to developed as well as to developing nations. In days of rapid and crucial decision, when mistaken social policies can destroy the environment and humanity, we need all the human resources we can get.

Psychological and sociological views of human potentiality are also reflected in a major strand in our religious tradition. Along with the view of man as repeated sinner, the Bible and the theology of the church have also emphasized man's capacity for high achievement. Out of his research in the New Testament, Ernest Cadman Colwell says of the excessively pessimistic humility that caricatures persons as wicked sinners, "There is often a dank cellar odor to this humility that is not found in Jesus." [30] Jesus showed us what we might become if we took seriously our relationship with God, becoming completely open or transparent to the ground of our being. The New Testament recognizes that human beings can become "partakers of the divine nature" (II Peter 1:4), "sons of God" or "children of God" (John 1:12–13; Rom. 8:14–23; Gal. 3:26 to 4:7; Phil. 2:15; I John 3:1–2). Any person can become "a new creation" (II Cor. 5:17). There can be such a wholehearted devotion to love and the purpose of God that sinlessness is a possibility (Matt. 5:48; Rom. 6:1–23; James 1:4; I John 3:5–9). It is even suggested that we will do greater works than Jesus (John 14:12) and that a future Spirit will guide us into a truth fuller than Jesus expressed (John 16:13). Even though one has not attained this, he can press on toward that goal

(Phil. 3:12–14; Eph. 4:13).

Recovery of this often-neglected strand in our tradition would include but also take us beyond the concept of God's forgiveness. The church and more gloomy theologians have often not gone farther than the "words of assurance" in a traditional worship service which assure us that we are forgiven and accepted as persons in spite of our sin. Religious emphasis during the future can do better than this. Forgiveness is deeply important to human growth. Emotional health requires recognition that we are still accepted as persons, in spite of some of our acts, and that the potentiality for a better life is still very much alive within us.

Always, however, religion makes a greater contribution when it goes beyond forgiveness to empowerment. God, through the structures of reality, is constantly supporting our capacities for greater perfection. In theological terms this goes beyond atonement (in which some divine act makes it possible for sin to be forgiven) to incarnation (in which the presence of God in a person makes it possible for good to be done). As W. Norman Pittenger has put it: "We need to revise our doctrine of man so that what classically is styled 'the Incarnation' illuminates human nature generally as well as describes Jesus Christ specifically." If such an enlargement is to be possible, "much that is in the theology, liturgies, hymn books and devotional writing of Christian ages must be struck out as unworthy of the God who is Love." [31] Persons can then become cocreators with God, cooperators with that dynamic process by which the highest values in the universe are actualized. Contrary to the cynic's complaint, our lives can leave much more of an imprint than scratching our signatures on chips of ice during a hot August day. In creativity we can find our full integrity, grandeur, and purpose for existence.

Highs and Superhighs in Ecstasy

Seeing ourselves for what we really are and responding to a view of the larger whole is the avenue to human ecstasy. Reality and ecstasy are likely to be unique emphases distinguishing the religion of the next decades partly because the most thorough satisfaction, wonder, and delight are possible only if they are based on what dependably exists. The word "ecstasy" is here used to refer to experiences of deep satisfaction and joy and well-being that are astonishingly intense and pervasive of the entire being. The world looks much different from usual, suffused by illumination, beauty, and meaning. Ecstasy involves "a standing outside of the taken-for-granted routines of everyday life." [32] At the same time the subject may feel himself inextricably related to all reality. There tends to be a greater transparency to truth as though the veils had been dropped or the barriers removed. Life is seen as an arena for enjoyment. Existence is not a burden or a punishment. If life seems dreary and boring, we have not become authentic human beings open to the whole of reality. Religion adds festive celebration, with color, dance, bells, and banners. These experiences of

the whole person, based both on cognitive insight
and emotional feeling, erupt into life with powerful impact, drawing the recipient out of his former
self into a new level of existence. In such peak experiences, to use a phrase from C. S. Lewis, we are
constantly "surprised by joy." [33]

The word "ecstasy" is colloquially used to describe the feeling accompanying sexual orgasm, or
a gourmet banquet, or a drug experience, or mind-
blowing rock festivals, or driving a big car, or
watching one's dividends accumulate. These activities often involved avoiding higher values or
deeper aspects of reality, or quieting some major
human capacities, or temporarily adding an artificial outside stimulus. Genuine ecstasy goes far
beyond this. Explosive or exciting as these lesser
delights may be, they are still decidedly minor by
comparison with the greatest ecstasies known to
humanity. The peak ecstasies are continuously
available under a wider variety of circumstances.
They endure for longer periods of time. They involve more of our basic nature and total personality, and they have a wider range of constructive
consequences. Instead of depending on external
crutches such as drugs, peak ecstasies are released
by nurturing permanently available inner resources. Ecstasy is fraudulent if it requires deadening human sensibilities or reducing contact with
reality. A flight from reality makes hope impossible. Realistically facing grim external circumstances is compatible with the highest ecstasies,
because they do not depend on fortunate conditions, material prosperity, or social applause. A

permanent "high" internally can persist even during low moments externally. Even during tragedy we can remain triumphant.

The greatest ecstasies known to humanity can be described under four headings. Most of us know something about these four because we have touched them gingerly in momentary flashes. We also know that other persons have made these, in varying degrees, the dominant tone of their entire lives.

The first of the more thoroughgoing ecstasies is the deep consciousness of self-discovery, knowing who I am and the meaning of my life in relationship to the whole of reality. This involves acceptance of myself as a person of worth and high potentiality. It embodies a deep awareness that I am at home in the universe, accepted by God. There is a remarkable activation of the ability to transcend the present self. There is a feeling of aliveness in all the positive aspects of personality, including some previously neglected. This is an experience of being in vibrant touch with one's feelings and intellect. Instead of being at war with oneself, this provides a central priority for life toward which all life's energy can be focused in a single direction. This is the kind of resource Kierkegaard was talking about when he said purity of heart is to will one thing. This makes possible the new being that Tillich stressed as the answer to human anxiety about meaninglessness. It is important to bring people to "realize where they are; what they are missing; what has happened to them; what they have lost; why they are lonely, in-

secure, anxious, without ultimate purpose, without
an ultimate concern, without a real self, and without a real world." [34]

This ecstatic realization has come to many with
great emotional power in a single central experience, like the conversion experiences in a religious
pilgrimage of some persons. To others, this may
come as more of a steady growth and sustaining
orientation of life, with repeated peak moments.
To all who have had it in one form or another
comes a dependable gift of grace liberating them
from the tyranny of convention and of material
things, and steadily sustaining an underlying adequacy and happiness through even the most negative conditions.

A second major ecstatic experience is that of at-
homeness in the whole of the natural world. Everyone has felt something of this at some luminous
moment standing under the stars or on a mountain
or in a garden. This includes getting in touch with
our bodies. We accept them as good, even though a
lesser good, and revel in the joy of touch and
movement. The rhapsodic representation of the
natural world may also come to us through great
music or art. When they really speak to us of
beauty and meaning, we can hear phrases from the
music of the spheres. Through nature or art we can
feel a unity with reality, in the sense not of identity
but of intimacy with elemental things, a feeling of
being an active part of a living universe.

Theodore Roszak speaks of man as "en-
capsulated in a *wholly* man-made environment,
sealed up and surviving securely in a plastic

womb." At the same time, satisfied with our accomplishments, we suffer "the overweening pride of the doomed." [35] We drive to a manicured version of nature in a park, take a transistor radio which drowns out the sounds and the silences of nature, and leave beer cans strewn around when we leave. We could be released from this desecration with its clutching for release from tension. We could in relaxation and wonder live closer to the soil, seeing signs of glory in the huge variety of grasses and rocks. We could experience the weather and feel ourselves in friendly relationship to galaxies in space. Or like Francis of Assisi, we could speak to the birds and refer to *Brother* Sun and *Sister* Moon.

All this can be consistent with a sense of priorities which sees the needs of men or the actualization of more inclusive values as more important than physical things. Yet we can immerse ourselves in the natural world as part of the whole of things that points us toward the ultimate. This was the connection made by an ancient psalmist, "Bless the LORD, O my soul! . . . (Thou) hast stretched out the heavens like a tent, . . . who makest the winds thy messengers. . . . Thou makest springs gush forth in the valleys. . . . O LORD, how manifold are thy works! In wisdom hast thou made them all." (Ps. 104.)

A third source of ecstasy is the experience of close relationship with other persons and especially the satisfaction that follows significantly helping someone else. An amazing sense of unity often astounds those who enter into fellowship that

is real, honest, and compassionate. An unparalleled
sense of fulfillment follows active expression of altruistic concern. This comes as an unsought consequence. If one helps another out of desire for personal ecstasy, the rapture is lost. Love is not
self-indulgence. Fulfillment comes when one em-
pathetically feels the other's pain and acts spontaneously to help even at painful cost to oneself.
Erik Erikson states this paradox in interpreting the
truth-force of Gandhi: "To be ready to die for what
is true now means to grasp the only chance to have
lived fully." [36] The insight of Jesus was, "Whoever
would save his life will lose it," but those whose
primary motivation is to invest life for a great cause
will find life abundantly (Matt. 16:25; Mark 8:35;
Luke 9:24; 17:33).

In one group therapy session, a woman who
claimed never to have been loved and who found
it hard to love started screaming: "What is love?
What is love?" After a few moments someone
quietly said: "Love is someone saying: 'Get out of
bed, it's time for school. Eat your vegetables. Take
your vitamins.'" [37] Love is that, and it is marching
in a picket line for justice for workers. Love is
working as a volunteer in a hospital, and it is writing a congressman to urge policies aiding poverty-
stricken peoples in the Third World.

A life-orientation toward the needs of other people is a direct contradiction to preoccupation with
personal ease in an affluent society. Outgoing service is also a direct contradiction of the self-centered acquisitive motive in economics and politics,
and of the impersonalism of urban life. Ecstasy that

follows really significant service is much different from the short-lived, superficial thrills following personal acquisition, as of a new car or of a new job with greater authority to dominate. The major ecstasy of which we are speaking goes considerably beyond that part of the human potential and growth group movement which gets mired down in personal titillation, shallow festivity, and egoistic expression of the self. Those are lost souls who in our generation have experienced a massive downsurge in social hope and who are running about in an erratic search for personal ecstasy. In trying to "turn on," they are turning in toward privatized inner experience. This may bring some limited gratification. But with respect to the deepest satisfactions, a selfish search for nirvana is contradictory and self-defeating. That road becomes a dead-end street. Without human compassion life is dismally empty and deformed. Men and women are so made that they find fulfillment in love.

The crowning ecstasy of all adds communion with God to community among persons. This is the experience of intimate relationship with whatever we consider the highest and the most whole in all reality. This is felt as an aliveness in the center of our being related to the central dynamic of the universe. This is what the mystics were talking about when they used such metaphors as "fire" or the "beatific vision." The mystical experience, in Tillich's quotable phrase, is "an experience of the presence of the infinite in the finite." [38] This encounter with God in a total involvement of life takes various forms for different people. Most of us have felt some such ecstatic experience of God momentarily when an experience of nature or other persons went beyond nature and persons to touch the whole of ultimate reality. We at that moment sensed to some degree that coming thoroughly alive to God could carry us far beyond the proper poses and stolid superficiality of people thronging the streets and even crowding the pews of a great many churches. This more intense feeling may also be experienced as a more continuous intimacy with God during one's work, family life, and all the other worthwhile activities of life. It may be a moving sense of well-being and assurance in problem-solving. It may be a rapt, effortless, imageless, mind-altering experience of peace and power, seemingly apart from other attachments. It may be a feeling of unity with all things. Whatever form it takes, this deeply moving experience of God is the most pervasive human ecstasy and accompanies the highest of all the priorities of life. According to Jesus, loving God with all one's being is "the great and first commandment" (Matt. 22:37–38; Mark 12:29–30).

There is abundant testimony that the experience of God enhances and intensifies each of the other forms of ecstasy. The first three forms may be thrilling experiences, but they do not become the fullest possible ecstasy until they are set in the framework of a view of God, until their partial disclosure is related to the totality of reality. The discovery of the self is even more satisfying when a person sees himself also as a spiritual being related to a cosmic plan. Relationship to nature is more significant when nature is perceived as a manifestation of God. Service to neighbor takes on a different quality when such service is measured against a higher standard of values, a more universal definition of neighbor, and the time span of eternity. These four ecstasies can partially be released through psychological counseling, growth groups, social movements, or nature clubs, but all of these lack the enlargement which is only possible through a religious perspective.

This combination of the religious dimension and the common life releases experiences higher than the "high" of which we ordinarily speak. These experiences may come as extraordinary occasions of wild joy. More often they are felt as calm and supportive healing and empowerment continuously permeating day-to-day life. This becomes a permanent "high" as well as a superhigh. It is vastly superior to the transient, externally stimulated feelings induced by drugs, sex, or escapist entertainment. A high school girl said it this way: "Since I have been involved in an awareness group in my church, I have had no desire for marijuana. . . . I can get really high on nature, books, music, and, most of all, people. It's beautiful!" Life then becomes festival, celebrating the goodness of existence. This is not life meager, but life abundant (John 10:10). Such an aliveness of authentic human capability is more than a match for the forces of antilife. This is one reason religion will never die out. It points the way toward the highest ecstasy combined with the greatest possible social helpfulness within a meaningful interpretation of the whole of reality. A vital meeting between God and man is the central feature in man's destiny.

There are good reasons for believing that this relationship also continues eternally. This further hypothesis may prove less convincing to many people. Such persons can still confidently hold to what has been said on previous pages even though they may not accept the extra bonus in the next paragraphs. I now turn briefly to the less substantiated but vitally intriguing possibility of ecstatic life even beyond death. What are the probabilities that we are now living in only one stage of eternal life?

As evidence points toward continuation of physical values and social legacies, though often in altered form, so personality and spiritual values may well continue beyond what we call death. What seems the end becomes then a greater beginning. If God preserves values, he would surely in some way preserve those in human personality, which are among the highest values we know. Seeing death as only an episode in continuous existence becomes more plausible as we are impressed by new scientific discoveries in the spiritual capacities of persons. There is empirical data pointing toward the extension of the functioning of persons beyond the space-time situations to which we have tended to limit them. It is not so strange as it once was to think of persons as living spirits also functioning apart from the body in which they are now set. We are accumulating more insights from (1) extrasensory perception, including telepathy between persons at a distance; (2) mystical experiences that seem to lift one above categories of time and space; (3) the development of Jung's concept of the group unconscious into the possibility that "everyone could be in touch with everything that has ever been known or thought"; [39] or (4) unexplained phenomena suggesting some kind of communication or influence upon us by the dead. Further research in the paranormal may prove some of these clues to be false. Others may be supported by increasingly convincing evidence.

Confidence in eternal life is also enhanced as we have strong religious experiences of close spiritual relationship with God. Such transcendent experiences develop strong confidence in the ultimate cosmic unity of all creation, in which forms may change, but all still remains a creative part of a dynamic universe. The transcendent dimension of reality persists regardless of changes in physical structures. Human personality as it reaches toward its full possibilities of sonship with God can share in this transcendent element in reality. For many people, when the idea of a beautiful and powerful personality, like that of Jesus, and the idea of death collide in their minds, it is the idea of death that is changed.

The threat of nothingness is further demolished by the probability of a higher range of vitality, a suprahuman or suprapersonal sphere of creativity. John Cobb suggests that one reason the believer in God is entitled to hope for life after death is that "the God who brought order into being out of chaos, novelty out of endless repetition, life out of subliving nature, man out of subhuman forms of

life, and the occasional saint out of a sinful humanity may also have the power to sustain or re-create
man in a quite new form." [40] The central power in
the universe gave us the surprise of life in the miracle of birth. It is not too strange to think that death
may also become birth, a transition from the womb
of this present world into a higher existence that
we are now too insensitive to imagine.

Whether or not we believe that life is eternal, we
still have ample reason to develop human potentialities to the full, here and now. It continues to be
extremely important to live life completely and to
make one's social influence as creative as possible
now and for future generations. If we believe, as
was pointed out in the preceding chapter, that our
actions even affect what God is able to do, then the
influence of our lives continues in some sense to
have universal dimensions.

The Resurgence of Religious Experience

Something that has been shut up under dust
covers in the attic is now beginning to be dis-
played as a prize possession. This rediscovered
treasure is religious experience. Quakers, now
sober and silent, once "quaked" for joy. Method-
ists, now stiff and formal, once reacted with open
enthusiasm and deep feeling. Modern expressions
do not need to be as flamboyant as some past manifestations. Our recovery of religious experience
can be just as genuine if it is quietly but power-
fully moving. In ways appropriate to our even
more thrilling resources, larger numbers of people

are now openly and honestly looking for a deeper relationship to the transcendent. "Jesus people" or Eastern religions are the current style in some parts of the youth culture. Adults also are swinging incense, chanting *"om,"* repeating mantras, attending revival meetings, practicing biofeedback. Prayer, meditation, mysticism, and charismatic experience have become respectable areas for exploration. Part of this is fad—the spiritual equivalent of the hula hoop. But part of this is a desperate cry of need. Church persons in larger numbers are recognizing that their own religious experience does not need to be so prosaic. Krister Stendahl, dean of Harvard Divinity School, spoke of our need for "high-voltage religion" to replace the common "flashlight-battery type of religion." [41] Our condition was described in Robert L. Johnson's metaphor, "We sniff around the rims of extinct volcanoes, but no lava flows, no fire burns." [42] We are setting out to rediscover fire.

The release of the full possibilities of the whole person awaits our being seized passionately by the deepest significance of reality. Since we have not been so seized, we are not so liberated. Birds sing, and we never hear them because we are listening to something else. Great books remain unread because we watch too many sports events. Stereo music can be substituted for times of concentrated thinking. Deep feelings are left unexpressed while we talk about the weather. Experiences of God are avoided while we enjoy a blank mind with our beer. We say that God is not broadcasting and all the time we have been tampering with the receiving apparatus. Triviality may be used as a protective shield against deep intimacy or loving relationships. Families at meals may talk about the dinner menu or a television program to avoid genuine sharing. The ritual element in worship may be used to ward off deeply shaking religious experience. Even eucharistic bread and wine may be misused to monopolize our attention with their historical background or with repentance for some personal peccadillo, so that we can avoid facing our responsibility for war or economic exploitation. In general we build protective barriers against unaccustomed stimuli to fulfillment, while we remain very energetic about deadening activities. We commit chronic suicide persistently throughout life, killing our most significant selves.

Some of our substitutes for religious experience are good, except when they stand in the way of something more important. It is a fantastic experience to have a gourmet meal by candlelight, but if that is the greatest satisfaction we ever have, we have scarcely begun to be human. Sex is wonderful, but if that is the greatest enjoyment we have, we remain substantially unawakened. Comic strips may be entertaining, but they scarcely have the same priority as the front page of *The New York Times*. The greatest barriers to self-realization are often not inherently evil acts, but good things given too great prominence. This was the meaning in the parable of Jesus about the great feast of the community of God, missed by people with good but comparatively trifling excuses. (Luke 14:15–24.) Lesser values, good in moderation, become evil in excess. The point of transmutation comes sooner when we emphasize higher priorities. We sooner consider ourselves gluttons instead of gourmets when we feel deep empathy with undernourished millions in the Third World. So it is with private material accumulation, weekend recreation, economic advancement, or the architectural embellishment of churches. All are good up to a point. Accurately seeing the point requires the perspective of total commitment to that which alone deserves ultimate loyalty. By its scrambling of priorities modern life in many ways has become a conspiracy against life. Its gifts may also be its poisons. Surrounded by material abundance, we still live in depressed areas. We have lost something very important but cannot remember what it is. With respect to our total beings we remain as handicapped as a quadriplegic. Lacking a religious dimension to personality, we exist as basket cases without arms and legs.

We do not need to remain unaware cripples. There is a cure for our condition. The major barriers to ecstasy and to a more loving society are our tendencies to consider religious experience as less important than even the unimportant, and to remain rigidly self-satisfied with an inferior style of life. The great prerequisites for religious experience become the opposites of these, namely: (1) to consider relationship with God important enough to spend more time on and (2) to remain open and teachable, ready for noticeable transformations of life-style. The first of these prerequisites reminds us that what we pay attention to is what we are affected by. The second prerequisite demands that we be alert to our own inadequacy, avoid defensive protection of imperfection, hold loosely to present prejudices, and welcome new insights. Reality is there, ready to be discovered and used. God can be depended upon. He offers us his gifts. It is only for us to reach out our hands to receive. Or to change the figure, the sun has come up and the light is there. We need only to raise the shades in our rooms.

These windows to transcendence appear constantly in daily life. But a resurgence of religious experience is not likely without specific times also being set aside for group worship and for private meditation. Devotional experience in both of these two forms can bring a vision of total reality, releasing power beyond our normal capacities, and introducing profound celebration into life.

Not every service of public worship does this. One lay person recently complained that "clichés are used as a substitute for substance." A college student said: "I want to leave church loving life. It's been a long time since a sermon made me feel good." To meet such deficiencies, new forms of contemporary worship are beginning to be widely used in churches. For many persons such new styles are providing more variety and spontaneity, greater freedom for the emotions, contemporary rhetoric, music, and symbols, a more intriguing view of God and a less dismal view of man, a more joyous and informal mood. Other persons find a more stirring experience in a more stately traditional setting. The vastness of God is so great and

our backgrounds so varied that one would expect
different persons to find vital meaning in different
forms of worship. The growing appreciation of
pluralism in our culture applies to religion as well.
We can use different approaches to worship without feeling that we must dogmatically defend the
superiority of one or the other for everyone.

One would expect a similar pluralism in private
religious experience. Again there are general common prerequisites and characteristics. Yet there is
no standard detailed pattern for the personal devotional life. The report of the monastic or of the
mystic must be taken seriously as he tries to describe ineffable episodes that can scarcely be put
into words. On the other hand there are homemakers, business persons, and industrial workers
who have experienced a steady serenity and satisfaction which seems less spectacular but may turn
out to be even more productive. A way of combining these two emphases in a particularly promising
approach will be discussed in a later section
headed "Sublimity in a Simple Setting." One of
the dangers in the present revival of interest is that
religious experience may be regarded as occult and
esoteric, when actually it is normal and universally
available.

Religious Experience and Belief in God

One of the strongest considerations supporting
the reality of God is the evidence of personal religious experience. Through the centuries persons
have had immediate awarenesses that seemed best

interpreted as the presence of God. Some would
say that in view of this widespread experience it is
not necessary to gather any further evidence. Since
we have such immediate awareness, they conclude
that argument for God's existence is no more called
for than are arguments for the existence of tables or
trees, which are directly noted by the senses. From
this perspective one might ask: Do you need proof
of God? Does one light a torch to see the sun? It
seems truer to the broadly scientific method of research, however, to say that religious experience
and other characteristics of reality reinforce each
other in suggesting the reality of God. Purely personal experiences may be misleading and misin-
terpreted. We had better ask whether other evidence also sustains the belief that ours is an
experience of God. Such other supporting evidence was discussed in the preceding chapter. The
feeling of relationship with God is a particularly
important argument when it is advanced in addition to other evidence and is not made to bear the
entire burden for sustaining belief.

Faith is more than intellectual assent or religious
experience. It is the complete response of the
whole person. Suppose that in an air raid a child in
an Asian village is hit by a bomb fragment. While
others are rushing about in confusion, the mother
cradles the child in her arms and feels intensely
the full brunt of the tragedy. An inquiring newspaper reporter uses all the techniques of logical inquiry—interviewing, observing, taking pictures. His
account may be more accurate than the mother's,
yet he understands less of what happened than

does the mother. A detached observer, lacking direct experience, does not have all the data. On the other hand, the mother needs the verdict of doctors and international statesmen before she fully knows what has happened to her. Personal experience and more comprehensive inquiry go together.

Some persons have had what Abraham Maslow out of his psychological research called "peak experiences" in the broad sense, apart from a view of the transcendent.[43] These persons can find their experiences even richer and more meaningful if they accept other evidence and relate their peaks to the transcendent dimension of God. Other persons have had nothing they interpret as religious experience but are convinced by other aspects of the nature of reality that there is such a transcendent dimension. As was pointed out in the previous chapter they can base life on that faith. The sun is there behind the clouds on a cold day even if I do not see it or feel it. But such believers can do better than merely intellectualize. By going outdoors over enough days they can also feel the sun. In the light of other theoretical considerations it looks as though there were a God. We try out the hypothesis and it works. Our hunch gets additional confirmation from religious experience. Arguments to support the existence of God finally become invitation to religious experience. Alert and open persons will want to grow in this area of life as well as in others.

In one form or another this expanded experience is available to every person. As Paul Tillich put it,

"Spiritual experience is a reality in everyone, as solid as the experience of being loved or the experience of the air one breathes." [44] The way may be prepared by a quiet but insistent realization that our lives are too empty and meaningless, but that the void within us can be filled. Religious experience may have its elementary beginnings in intellectual inquiry, aesthetic experience, human intimacy, or ethical action. Then it joins and magnifies all of these into a sublime and luminous whole. There is available emotional power to shake us loose from the mediocrity of the average day and to lift us above dullness and disaster. To be human means to be able to perceive something ultimate, to receive some word about the dimension of the transcendent. The authentic human heritage of peace, power, and perspective can be claimed. There are resources to carry us far beyond the profanity of normal existence into a quality of life that makes everything new.

Sublimity in a Simple Setting

One feature of a religion for the future, much stressed in these pages, is that it will be rooted in the common life. God is an aspect of reality. Religion is a way of life that relates normal activities to the transcendent. This has important implications also for personal religious experience in its more advanced stages.

The development of devotional experience has been described in terms of a ladder of prayer. One begins on the lower rungs and then mounts to what has sometimes been called "high prayer." This has usually been considered as some form of contemplation, thought of as an imageless feeling of ecstatic union with God, including the experience of the classical mystic. For many persons this may indeed be the peak of the devotional life. Having gone through the verbal expression of vocal prayer or the train of thought of meditation, they enter into this freely given torrent of sensation which brings intuitive insight, unifying power, deeper radiance, and calm serenity. Those of us who have experienced such brief moments of incandescence may well wish more prolonged periods of this "inward refreshment" and "loving attentiveness toward God," as St. John of the Cross described it. There is something to be gained from the stilling of competitive claims, the dying to the old self, the detachment from egocentric interests, and the quiet simplicity of waiting that are included in preparation for the gift of contemplation. This does not have to become escapist or world-denying. It may contribute a great deal to human fulfillment.

There is, however, another form of "high prayer" that may become more characteristic of modern persons. It constitutes a somewhat different approach to the mystical experience. This peak experience in personal devotional growth is "the practice of the presence of God," to use the classical designation by Brother Lawrence. As a cook in a Carmelite monastery, Brother Lawrence could say, "The time of business does not with me differ from the time of prayer; and in the noise and clutter of my kitchen, while several persons are at the same time calling for different things, I possess God in as great tranquility as if I were upon my knees at the blessed sacrament." [45] In effect, washing dishes had become another form of taking communion, and the clatter of pots and pans could become organ and choir. He had learned to relate all that he did to the ultimate meaning in God. He continuously merged worship and work in such a way as to lift his total life to a more ecstatic level. This did not eliminate concentrated periods of worship, meditation, or prayer, but it had the effect of extending such a devotional period through the entire day.

For us there are still times for standing back and reflecting, but these moments are not particularly "holy" or "religious." "Spiritual exercises" include action in the world also. This is an expression of the beyond in the midst which is so characteristic of modern religious thought. The holy is a dimension of everything that is real. God comes in the common life of working, eating, playing. It is the appropriation of a new quality of life which moves human potentiality toward its divine fulfillment. It makes religion at once thoroughly realistic and thoroughly transforming. Instead of letting the multiplied activities of life crowd God out, we take God into them. The unchanging environment of our lives becomes the whole and the ultimate. We now live in constant awareness of the continuous, pervasive presence of God.

The meaning of this approach becomes clearer in the suggestion often made for nurturing the experience—that we practice it deliberately and periodically until it becomes spontaneous and continuous. That is to say that we repeatedly, consciously recall the highest we know, or God, while we go about our normal routine. There is a beautiful expression of this in the story of Jesus walking with unknown friends to Emmaus. As he broke the bread for their eating together, they recognized who Jesus was, and the entire experience was transformed (Luke 24:13–35).

For example, one might momentarily recall God at particular times during the day, as the first thing in the morning, or before meals, or at the beginning of each coffee break. Or one might think a very brief "ejaculatory" or "javelin" prayer at certain places on one's accustomed route. A selected tree can each day be a reminder to give thanks for beauty. A particular house can remind us of the needy families of the world. Passing a school can be a call to prayer for peace: "O God, help me to do something to make this world safe for children." Or there can be a brief direction of attention in connection with various activities. Washing one's hands can be a reminder of the need for inner purification and integrity. Entering one's office or turning on one's machine may become also instantaneous meditation on the high purpose of our vocation. Sitting down in a movie or answering the telephone might all have their appropriate thrusts of "javelin" prayer. Allan Hunter suggests that every time we are with a person we silently say, "For his sake I consecrate myself"—which would always considerably improve our attitude toward persons.

We condition children, whenever they see a box of matches, to think of the consequences of fire, or adults in observing a pack of cigarettes to think of the possibilities of cancer. When we see blackberries in the woods many of us think of jam. So when we see a sentence in a book or the headlines in the newspaper, should we not think of God's criteria of truth and responsibility? Education consists of seeing deeper and truer significance in human events. Religion can likewise relate the deepest and truest of all perspectives to every human experience.

Some of this sounds silly and artificial. The purpose, however, is not legalistic or pedantic. It is rather the enlargement of all experience, placing it in its total setting. Many have found that after a time, the deliberate practice becomes unnecessary and that increasingly a new consciousness spontaneously remains with them. The ordinary becomes extraordinary. Life as a whole is changed. Some activities are eliminated or subordinated. Others are introduced or expanded in our time schedules. We feel and act differently. We live the unified life in which the highest direction we know is related to everything we do. When on his deathbed Thoreau was asked whether he had made his peace with God, he replied, "I was not aware that we had quarreled."

Religion is a transforming quality of life instead of an isolated segment of existence. God is everywhere. We miss seeing God only because we close our eyes. Every time we step on the earth, we might remember the dependability of an ordered universe. Every time you touch your skin or touch anything, there is evidence of the power that sustains all being. Whenever I see a building or see anything, I might be reminded of a pervasive process of creativity. Whenever we flex our muscles, focus our eyes, or think a thought, we might do so in a framework of awareness of the amazing nature of unrealized potentialities. Every time we experience either happiness or sadness, we might be conscious of the personal warmth of love at the heart of a living universe. Truly religious persons delight in the world and celebrate the secular because here they meet ultimate goodness and love. Having had in the world a full, vibrant experience of God, they find the world apart from God lukewarm, tepid, empty, and boring.

All worthwhile human experience can be religious experience if it is related to the most ultimate concern. The danger is that we overlook the last half of that statement. There are great possibilities in a merger of the sacred and the secular, so long as the secular does not become the dominant partner. Religion always introduces a distinctive element into any person's life-style. Meditation involves thinking, but it is more than mere thinking. Meditation is thinking within the frame of reference of God and his purposes. All worthwhile reading can become devotional reading, if we look for luminous phrases that let the light of ultimate meaning shine through. Many thoughts can become prayers if they are expressions of aspiration or confession or thanksgiving or dedication to God. "To labor is to pray" if work is carried on as the calling of God. Behavior can become a form of worship to the extent that it expresses a distinctive preoccupation with creativity beyond the conventional. That is the subject of the next chapter.

4

EMANCIPATION BY ACTION

There are many ways of being irreligious in the name of religion. One of the most common is to contradict in conduct what is professed in principle. We rationalize personal luxury as making us more fit to act compassionately toward the poor. Or we label as unrealized ideal what is actually widely practiced mediocrity. It has been suggested that our culture might be described as Christianity plus the conveniences. When the two become contradictory, we revise the Christianity rather than reduce the conveniences. The authentically religious person leads an exposed life of creativity out where the most traffic is moving or the worst bombs are falling. Yet most of us want martyrdom only on a foam-rubber cross. The so-called civil religion, which Robert Bellah finds widespread in the United States,[46] simply gathers up some of the commendable generalizations, like freedom and opportunity, commonly accepted from our national heritage though still often denied in our present practice. This is a false religion in that it falls far short of the full meaning of the transcendent dimension of reality. By breeding self-satisfaction it actually interferes with real confrontation with genuine religion.

Appropriate action is probably the aspect of religion which is most unwanted. Many of us reject religion not so much because we have intellectual difficulties with it but because we are unwilling to pay the ethical price. It may be true that it is impossible for us to find meaning in outdated theological forms, but it may also be true that there is a deeper problem inside ourselves. Some of our criticisms of the church may be projections of our own inadequacies.

The Indispensability of Ethics

Many of us keep ethics and religion around for decorative purposes only, like antique chairs in a museum meant to be looked at but not sat on. At the same time, important sections of the population are now demanding a more robust religion that takes behavior alteration seriously. Many young people are sincere when they insist, "The church will have to show me it means business before I will give it a second thought." This group of young people is rebelling against compromises made by recent generations with war, poverty, pollution, and dehumanization. Indeed they should rebel against such easygoing prolongations of infamy! When thoughtful adults also see religion for what it really is, they become unwilling simply to sit and talk about the problems. As one homemaker said, "I want to quit all this talking and do something about at least one of the problems in my society." As the cultural crisis continues to deepen, as education and expectations continue to explode around the earth, as interest in potentialities for ecstasy and creative love in world religions continues to grow, the number of activists is likely to multiply considerably. Then, as Robert K. Hudnut said of the immediate future: "A do-nothing church just simply is not going to be tolerated. . . . Ask the young. Ask the poor. Ask the black. Ask the world." [47]

Those frustrated by mere preparatory talk are right in their demand for other forms of ethical action. Both personal fulfillment and social survival depend upon right action. Personal integrity is destroyed to the extent that one's conclusions are not supported by consistent conduct. The quality of personal life is diluted. We block self-realization and throw up barriers against peak experiences of ecstasy. Certain kinds of action are essential to highest self-fulfillment. Things are made that way. A tug-of-war with God or with the nature of reality is not a promising undertaking. Reality is such that enough poison brings death, and less poison leads to illness. We must breathe some pure air or we die. We must breathe enough pure air or we become sick. So it is necessary to love or we die to the higher ranges of human personality. It is necessary to love enough or we suffer sickness or crippling morally and spiritually and even physically.

To avoid the empty life of a typical suburbanite, the prescription is spontaneous outgoingness toward God in enriching religious experience, and positive action that makes an altruistic contribution to other persons. The two central directives or "great commandments" of Jesus called for expression of the whole self in love toward God and toward neighbor (Matt. 22:37–40; Mark 12:29–31; Luke 10:27–28). This is the central secret of the fulfilled life. People are fully free only to the extent that they rise up against the limiting conditions of their environment and in some significant way participate in the making of history. Men and women are inadequate as persons and they miss the higher ranges of ecstasy if they are uninterested in restraining social evil and if they are contented with present programs to meet human needs. Their creative potentialities atrophy and their outgoing initiative disappears. We choose to become prisoners, confined and deteriorating in our cramped cells, which may be comfortably upholstered but still have bars at the windows.

Right action is a necessity not only for personal existence and growth, but also for the survival of civilization and of mankind as a whole. Chief Justice Earl Warren made the widely reported suggestion that from among clergymen and others we needed to develop a profession of counselors in ethics, just as we have helpfully multiplied marriage counselors. He pointed out that when new business ventures are undertaken, all kinds of experts are consulted save one, the specialist in ethics who can speak to the social usefulness or righteousness of the plan. Unless there are such revolutionary expansions in the thinking of business executives, labor leaders, politicians, and other influential persons, Justice Warren saw it as obvious that we would bring on ourselves "quite avoidable disaster." [48]

The life of all future generations depends on basic social changes now in areas like international relations, ecology, and economic justice. Selfishness, indifference, or mistaken aims about these matters will lead to irreversible disaster for the entire earth. The death of God in politics precedes the death of politics. Social apathy becomes a form of treason to one's country and the world.

In the history of Christianity there have been various shifts in emphasis between faith and worship on the one hand, and personal and social action on the other. We now live in a time of convergence of basic social choices that must be simultaneously and rapidly made. Our conduct may be decisive for the future of mankind. Under present circumstances religious groups would do well to place a greater emphasis on works than has been common recently. Of course, belief is basic, God's grace always gives us more than we deserve, and we still need to avoid unjustified pride in what we do. But too overpowering an emphasis on grace can become a social opiate. Any religion that leaves difficult worldly things to God, while its devotees simply enjoy personal euphoria and forgiveness, is not much help to the enterprise of God in the modern world. Authentic religion requires a new quality in total life. Therefore there is no faith divorced from works. A fresh reading of the Bible can impress us with the great emphasis given to right conduct. Action was a test of the adequacy of religion. The Bible constantly linked worship and behavior. Isaiah had God say, "Is not this the fast that I choose: to loose the bonds of wickedness, to undo the thongs of the yoke, to let the oppressed go free . . . ?" (Isa. 58:6). Both the prophets and Jesus saw it as impossible to worship worthily until one had first acted on his or her social obligations (Amos 5:21–24; Matt. 5:23–24). Dag Hammarskjöld reflected this in saying, "In our era the road to holiness necessarily passes through the world of action." Rabbi Abraham Heschel once remarked, "When I marched with Martin Luther King in Selma, Alabama, I felt my legs were praying."

How to Decide What to Do

A sensitive person is never without questions about the best decision or action. Should I start taking vitamin pills? With the depletion of oil reserves is this trip worth driving a gas-guzzling private car? Who deserves my vote for mayor? The caring person makes decisions of this sort by relating the best he knows to even the least he does. That is, he holds goals in one hand—the highest and most ultimate he has been able to apprehend. In the other hand he holds the most detailed analysis he is able to make of even the most ordinary decisions of life. Then he brings the two hands together. This is another illustration of merging the transcendent and the common. It is again the dimension of the unrealized and the beyond in the midst of our lives.

The goals or outcomes we want for action are best derived from a holistic view of the totality of experience through the ages, to the fullest extent we are able to come by this. We conclude that stealing is generally bad because of what human experience shows to have resulted from it. Whether these results are good or bad depends also on our answer to the most ultimate questions about the meaning of life, the character of God, or the purpose of creation. Our most ultimate goals or norms are therefore derived from our theology. Without a healthy theology there is no sound ethical decision. General norms or directions for movement are elaborated in somewhat greater detail in principles or guidelines. These include such emphases as sincerity, loving regard for every individual, freedom, equal opportunity, brotherhood, or peace. Most persons, including saints and sinners and politicians of all persuasions, would loudly proclaim their acceptance of such a list of generalizations, whether or not their conduct is always consistent.

Any decision also involves a more or less well-informed view of the nature of the choice to be made, the alternatives open, and the consequences of each option. An intelligent opinion about foreign policy requires some knowledge of what nations are about, of the two or three general approaches we might use (such as military deterrence or international organization or attempted isolation), and of their probable consequences. If we act wisely, we then choose that alternative the consequences of which come closest to the goals or norms we hold.

Sound decision-making requires the wisdom of ethics and of theology, as in the Bible and in other historical sources, to illuminate our norms, and also the findings of natural and behavioral scientists to sharpen our view of options and of their consequences. We need both Quakers and statisticians, accomplished mystics and competent businessmen, Jesus as well as political scientists. As human problems become more complex we may well use quantitatively more of the latter, but qualitatively the former are more basic. Whenever churches, in their sermons or educational materials, resist including proportionately more data from the natural and behavioral sciences, they are endangering their own message because they deprive it of practical meaning. On the other hand, whenever secularists exclude the theological dimension, their policies become self-defeating because they are based on immediate and incomplete data.

The most adequate decision is made with full regard for the realities of the situation within which we must act. It is usually not possible to do what is theoretically perfect. Our options are limited by several factors. Finite man is physically unable to do everything. Actions of other people frequently block what we otherwise might do. Or several values, like freedom and order, may be involved in the same situation, and one must be minimized insofar as the other is maximized. In order to stay in business and supply quality products to consumers, a businessman may be forced to some compromises by unscrupulous competitors. A nation dedicated to peace also faces aggressors. Statesmen will energetically look for better ways than traditional policies, but no new policy is going to be perfectly pure. The point is that moral action is always of necessity the best possible action under the circumstances. We are to choose that option in the world of reality which moves us closest to the goals intended—and which should also thereby improve our chances of a better choice in the future. In ambiguous situations the tension between norm and act is never to be eased, neither by making the goal less radical nor by evaluating any human response more highly than it deserves. This dynamic view again stresses the importance of a transcendent dimension or religious loyalty within existing realities to impel us with imagination and initiative beyond comfortable rationalizations and easy compromises.

Is Religion Necessary for Morality?

The question might first be reversed. Is morality necessary for religion? What was called religion has often been used as a defense of currently accepted exploitation. This heresy seems especially acceptable to a church that has vast institutional holdings of property and prestige to be protected. Or emphasis on the personal comforts provided by religion may silence its uncomfortable social demands. Quoting Harvey Cox, this becomes a religion which "like the worst of the old pietism, allows people to profit blissfully from institutionalized injustice as long as they are warm and open with the individuals they meet personally." [49] This finally becomes the death of both comfort and religion. A religion related to reality must very prominently include ethics.

On the other hand, religion makes a unique and indispensable contribution to morality. Part of this gift of religion has already been suggested, especially in Chapter 2. The most adequate definition of direction or goals requires raising the ultimate and the holistic questions. The degree of commitment to these goals, also a religious matter, goes a long way in determining how compromised or how heroic action will be. Religion gets life all together. Personalities become more powerful insofar as they point in a single direction, rather than pull in several directions at once. Religion is properly defined as a way of total life, adding acting to thinking and feeling. The religious person goes beyond a view of reality to a response to reality. Outward conduct accords with inner conviction, and both fit into the total structure of things.

This perspective deepens motivation and persistence, qualities badly needed in facing the opposition and conflict inevitable in times of major change. Those can better stand firm who see their goals to be rooted in reality as a whole. That which is right is discovered in the way things are. That which is considered wrong or unjust goes against the grain of the universe. Things are to be taken more seriously if they are part of the ongoing process of an interrelated living universe or if we see ourselves as working with God to make possible the realization of his purposes.

Such a sense of destiny stimulates the thorough transformation of personal life which is essential to well-functioning social institutions. Even the best organized economic or political structures can be wrecked by deficient personnel running them. Simple honesty is a commodity in short supply in trade. Politics needs a massive transfusion of integrity. Crime in the streets—and in the homes at income tax time—leaves no one safe. What good will it do us to learn to produce offspring through the formula of our choice, if all we want in the next generation is 10 percent like Einstein, 5 percent like father, 5 percent like mother, and 80 percent like John Wayne? It is not enough to tack a thin veneer of sex education or budget training or psychological skills in communication on a fundamentally selfish core of character. Sex relations were in a mess when we were uptight about talking about sex. They are still in a mess when we are frank and permissive. Liberating relationships between the sexes is fundamentally a matter of sound religious and ethical orientation. Industrialists who mistake bigger piles of gadgets for quality and for joyousness of life are a menace to the resources of the planet. Artists without religious discernment provide a very deceptive view of existence.

Science without ethical sensitivities produces doomsday machines.

It is an outrageous waste of resources to engage in research simply because it is personally intriguing or because a research grant is available. Such uncritical motivations have implemented projects aimed at overkill in weaponry, overdevelopment of wasteful luxuries, or exorbitant profits for selfish-interest groups. The most socially productive guide to the use of resources is neither chance curiosity nor gross cupidity but responsible caring for the most important needs of persons. Even climbing Mount Everest only "because it is there" is an immoral act so long as there are families in nearby countries without a home and starving on the sidewalks. Without the prioritizing contribution of religion, knowledge becomes foolishness and our most magnificent achievements are perverted to massive failures. We thus exemplify Santayana's definition of fanaticism: "redoubling your effort when you have forgotten your aim."

Keeping action on target requires clarity about three basic questions: What values do we want? For whom do we want them? For how long a time? We properly ask questions like: What is important in life? What is most worth giving up other things for? To how many neighbors should love extend? Should we sacrifice for persons outside the family? Outside the United States? Beyond this generation? Science, as we usually think of it, does not speak to these questions. Computers remain silent and test tubes do not handle the data.

Introducing the transcendent dimension alters

the answers we give to the basic questions of which values, for whom, and how long. Secular ethics already answers these questions by stressing higher values, altruistically sought for others in the long run. Religion contributes to even more valid ethical conclusions because it enlarges or radicalizes all three of these considerations. Religion places greater stress on even higher spiritual values beyond the material and the social. It enlarges the circle of neighbors to include every person on earth and in all future generations. It extends the long run to include dimensions of eternity. This extends the claim of love and enlarges the concept of fulfillment of persons, which is the goal to be sought. Instead of looking superficially at what is immediately most evident, it invites attention to the whole and the ultimate.

This enhancement of goal is especially important when lower aims disintegrate against the realities of the universe. When experience finally shows us that there is no enduring thrill in accumulating gadgets or that there is no more titillating encore beyond a certain point in sex, then comes an ominous moment of decision. We can then give up the partial values in which we had trusted, and turn to nihilism and despair, or we can begin to emphasize a higher order of values. It would seem more sensible and more enjoyable to do the latter—and that is just what religion helps us to do.

Long human experience indicates that the most important as well as the most radical guide to action is the norm of love. Jesus expressed the greatest of all commandments in terms of love. (Matt.

22:37–40; Mark 12:28–31; Luke 10:25–28.) The climax of the incomparable thirteenth chapter of First Corinthians is, "But the greatest of these is love." Other major world religions join in a similar emphasis. There is widespread agreement among religious persons that "he who does not love does not know God" (I John 4:8).

Central emphases of entire disciplines in the behavioral sciences now move in a similar direction. Educational theory, psychotherapy, industrial relations, and criminology have all moved beyond former practices of coercive deterrence that kept the rod in the schoolroom and the goon squads in the factory. In a more individualized problem-solving approach, research in these fields now places much greater emphasis on a climate of acceptance, understanding, and recognition of the legitimate interests of the other. This is not yet the full expression of complete love, but all these findings of the psychological and social sciences move in that direction. When these discoveries are disregarded we reap the poisoned harvest of crime, mental illness, economic waste, and social disorder.

Love is informed, active concern for the full actualization of all others. It is responsible rather than naïve action; it is realistically informed by the relevant data. Love is the whole response of one's being, directed toward the highest welfare of those loved. Love is the victory of goodwill over estrangement, and of altruism over egoism. Love is inclusive, without boundaries of nation, class, race, or culture. As Kierkegaard suggested, it is impossible to give an incorrect answer to the question,

"Who is my neighbor?" Name any person whatsoever, and your answer is right. As in the parable of the good Samaritan (Luke 10:25–37), it is human need that alone is sufficient stimulus to release the action of love. The loving person pays particular attention to those in great need—the poor, the oppressed, the underprivileged, the spiritually undernourished, the neglected. Love accepts an unlimited liability. Action is to be carried to the point of sacrifice if necessary. This is not self-sacrifice, because the self is enhanced thereby. But wherever necessary, it is giving up those personal desires which are inconsistent with more important needs of others. High religions have seen this capacity for suffering love as a source of the triumphant power of God himself. Whatever one's precise Christology is, it puts in one form or another what Nietzsche called the "audacious inversion" of the concept "God on the cross."

The compassionate community, described in these radical terms, is the goal toward which we are to move as rapidly as possible. We may fail either because of too poor a program or too slow a speed. If we do follow the leading of love in the comprehensive and thoroughgoing fashion now both required by culture and emphasized by religion, we will find ourselves considerably beyond conventional morality. "Love your enemies" and "take up your cross" drop into present-day life as ideological bombs. Rollin Walker used to say that we have moderated Jesus' lightning flashes into safety matches. Finding the demand of the cross unbearable, we have invented formulas to excuse us from its imperative. Thereby we have lost the personal and social benefits of love.

How can such radical altruism be supported except by religious commitment? Less motivated persons may grudgingly make limited concessions when major crisis strikes. When scarce gasoline hits a dollar a gallon, they may buy a smaller car. That delayed and limited reaction is no longer enough to fit the facts. On several basic and indispensable changes it is too late for continued hesitation and half-measures. The times demand a more forward-looking citizenry, healed of its moral and religious anemia. The only way we can pull through our unprecedented combination of threats is with a deep change in consciousness and lifestyle. Action without a transcendent dimension will prove to be futile. Our most basic crisis is moral and spiritual. Constructively coping with our emergency is obstructed by antireligious tendencies. Nonreligious persons are actually refusing to consent to their own survival.

The Immorality of Current Morality

What is labeled as moral in our culture is often grossly immoral. Practices widely accepted as virtuous often turn out to be vicious. This is the kind of tragic reversal of values of which Isaiah spoke: "Woe to those who call evil good and good evil, who put darkness for light and light for darkness. . . . As the tongue of fire devours the stubble, and as dry grass sinks down in the flame, so their root will be as rottenness, and their blossom go up like dust." (Isa. 5:20, 24.) By adopting the immoral as though it were moral, we assist our own assassins. We seek safety by leaping into the jaws of destruction. This attempt to advance by retreat requires a cultural about-face.

One illustration of a good that becomes evil is the drive to ever-greater material production. As long as we lacked a lengthy list of necessities, this could be defended. Now increased production of material luxury that diverts scarce resources from necessities for the poor or for future generations is no longer progress but regression. Yet we still applaud those who invent and produce new luxury items. To get more wealth we use methods that destroy wealth in waste and in pollution of wealth-producing resources.

Or, to protect international peace, probably a majority of the American people support policies of nuclear deterrence and unilateral defense of our national interests. These policies maintain conflicts of interest with no final way to resolve them except by appeal to force. Many experts see these traditional aspects of policy as contributing to war rather than to peace. Or, for another illustration, the Watergate scandals showed how many politicians considered it justice to do injustice. Or, in a kind of intellectual mugging of the entire population, they thought it informing to tell lies. Political extremism in order to protect freedom has acclaimed methods that undermine freedom. It is a widespread American conviction that the acquisitive motive is the best way to contribute to social welfare, in spite of increasing evidence pointing to

the social costs of selfishness. We have long considered it good to help other people by dominating
them, but the exploited victims of imperialism or
racism or sexism see our "benevolence" in a different light. In antiquity, civilization was held on
the backs of millions of slaves. Today our standard
of living is partly supported by the sweat and sor-
row of millions in other lands. A "good Samaritan"
type of service to others now means nonviolent
revolution, in the sense of rapid, fundamental alteration of long-neglected patterns of exploitation.
We may delay on some things. We can deceive
ourselves with dreams. But there is no monkeying
around with masses of the poor or with nuclear ra-
diation or with the disruption of photosynthesis or
with an imbalance between population and natural
resources.[50]

Examples could be multiplied showing that what
we call wisdom often turns out to be exceedingly
unwise. Our most intelligent people, trained in
leading graduate schools, have brought on our
Vietnams. "How could we have been so stupid?"
asked President John F. Kennedy after he and his
advisers—one of the greatest arrays of intellectual
talent in American political history—had blun-
dered through the Bay of Pigs invasion. We have
called partial specialization omitting the religious
dimension "good," when in reality it easily becomes a form of evil until we make provision for
specialization plus a broad background self-con-
sciously and openly including the contributions of
religion.

Oversimplification is especially tragic since enough knowledge is available from the physical and social sciences on the one hand and from theology and ethics on the other to point general directions toward ways out of our dilemmas. We have more problems than we need to have and more solutions than we are actually using. While numerous details are not yet clear we can see that the extension of domestic freedom now requires more participatory democracy over a wider range of general policy decisions by an educated citizenry. In economic life we badly need new and less materialistic goals, a drastic reduction in inequalities of opportunity, and well-selected social controls for the common welfare. In ecology there are methods available to reduce pollution and the depletion of resources. A new style of life may reduce material standards of living but increase time for higher interests, netting a great step forward in human development. The relationships between nations can be less violent if we place greater reliance for protection on world organization, economic development of undeveloped nations, and diplomacy at the overlap of common aims.[51]

Once society condoned the whips and chains of respectable slave owners. Now these instruments are considered shockingly immoral. We can hasten the day when we will consider equally immoral bombing planes and hand grenades, elegantly equipped mansions, and laws to protect exorbitant incomes at the expense of the poor. We can contribute either to blasting civilization apart or to constructing a new era of justice, opportunity, and human fulfillment. The positive outcome will require drastic changes. In each case these changes turn out to be expressions of love in a larger degree. They are changes that have been advocated for years by socially concerned scholars and by church leaders, though without impressive support from masses of citizens or church members.

Not long ago I attended a church that printed as the first sentence of its morning prayer of confession, "Most of us do not come to you today with great, gross headline sins, our Father." Instead, the prayer went on to say, ours have been the failures of doubt, despair, and lack of personal helpfulness. These are lies! So long as we keep repeating such falsehoods in our prayers, so long will we remain personally stunted and socially threatened by disaster! Most of us are involved in huge deadly sins. Everyone who paid income tax during the Vietnamese conflict was an accessory to the bombing of babies. No matter how much we argued against the war or wrote our congressmen, our consciences cannot be entirely clear. Even those who believed the war the best possible policy under limiting international circumstances could reduce their guilt only if they were also actively supporting a peace organization working to change the international circumstances. While they never mugged anybody, everyone who uses expensive cosmetics or pet food, or by following style changes wastes outdated clothes, is diverting resources. Thereby they rob other peoples, contributing to malnutrition in poverty-stricken countries containing two thirds of the world's population. Everyone who, beyond what is absolutely necessary for sanity-preserving recreation, uses time in bridge, television viewing, sports attendance, or trivial conversation, and therefore less time in working against crime in the city streets or for forward-looking political reforms, is in actual fact cooperating with the Mafia and reactionary politicians. The removal of our influence from opposition to social enemies is one very important way of increasing their strength. If we do not support progressive political candidates, we make it easier for reactionaries to be elected.

In our particular cultural situation we might expand the medieval lists of seven deadly sins thought to bring damnation. My nomination for such a modernized list of seven devastating personal characteristics would be mediocrity, apathy, triviality, immediacy, privatism, insensitivity, and conformity. These become especially virulent in view of the unique characteristics of our cultural situation. We face complex, basic social change, stand at the edge of amazing new actualizations of human potentiality, and rely on more democratic decision-making processes which require participation. Under such circumstances it is fatal to bow to mediocrity and oversimplification, whether in television commercials, political analysis, or the poetic sentiments of youth. We dare not allow the comforts of affluence to entice us from necessary tedious training or difficult work. Our generation is called to be mightily achievement-oriented about eliminating war and poverty. This contrasts sharply with our common relapse from activism into apathetic acquiescence, whether in weekend boats or campers, or in communes in the hills, or in purely interior religion. Our priorities are in disarray so long as we magnify comparatively unimportant matters, whether abundance of sex or of wealth. Both appear rather trivial when compared with the full range of reality or with the cruel anguish of exploited millions around the world. Egoistic preoccupation with private gains becomes self-destructive, whether in the old style economic individualism or the new style self-expression. Our most serious energy crisis may turn out to be the withdrawal of human energy from the demanding decisions of our times.

The grip of these common characteristics becomes the more threatening because conformity to one's group is such a widely used security blanket. Both residents of a commune and junior executives in a corporation adopt the clothing styles and behavioral eccentricities of their peers with approximately equal fervor. In only somewhat different form, the seven sins being discussed are widely accepted by both dominant culture and counter-culture. Characteristics here listed as deadly are considered desirable by a large section of the population. As G. K. Chesterton suggested, the greatest of all illnesses is imagining that we are quite well. Tracing the social consequences of these seven widespread characteristics constitutes a road map for a descent into hell.[52]

Fulfillment Through Creativity

High religion points to better roads on the map and offers different personal characteristics. The religious dimension for action introduces thrilling openings for individual transmutation, in the dictionary sense of a change in basic nature that seems almost miraculous. When penitents came to the mourners' bench in brush arbor camp meetings, they expected a complete change to come over their life, and often it did. We now know that such changes can come gradually as well as suddenly—and that for modern complex times we can expect an even more thorough change than did the revivalists. In their day they were too often content with only the emotional rather than the rational aspects of personality also. They tended to stress improvements in simple interpersonal relationships and not the full range of attitudes and actions we now see to be necessary in a liberating society. As Harvey Cox puts our modern insight, "Interiority arises within us only as community emerges amidst us, and vice versa." [53] But our forefathers had something in the call to conversion. This is part of the essence of religion which we dare not tone down. Awakening to the religious dimension does introduce a deep crisis or turning point into life. Goals and priorities are shifted, and therefore all action directed toward them is altered. When we say "yes" to one dominant pattern for life, we must say "no" to another. Such a radical change and drastic commitment is indispensable for the full flowering of new life.

This mutation is to a life-style quite different from the ordinary. The typical has not been good enough. If we contentedly accept anything that exists in self or society, we can be sure that we are denying the full will of God at that point. As Moltmann put it, "Peace with God means conflict with the world." [54] To become this kind of a nonconformist takes a measure of heroism. To join the minority requires a readiness to do without the applause of the majority. Dominant groups do not with conspicuous regularity reward their just critics. An outstanding Latin-American theologian, Gustavo Gutiérrez, reminds us, "The point is not to survive, but to serve." [55] Jesus went so far as to say, "Woe to you, when all men speak well of you" (Luke 6:26). But rapturously happy are "those who are persecuted for righteousness' sake" (Matt. 5:10). This is because the blessedly happy are absorbed in more important matters than persecution. The deep comfort that they experience comes not by avoiding struggle, but rather in the midst of conflict. Such renewed people are spontaneously responding to the central vitality of the universe and struggling to liberate other persons whose anguish they deeply feel. The extra unsought bonus that comes with their way of life is a deeper ecstasy than even the favors of the rich and powerful can provide.

Any religions suitable for the beginning of the twenty-first century must sponsor unconventionally creative lives. Such creativity manifests a more durable and intense quality of caring between persons in day-to-day considerateness and helpfulness. In an impersonal world, neglected and distressed people deserve immediate aid. Any adequate religion will also nurture greater vigor and skill in performing major life functions in the family, on the job, and in community citizenship. If we now really love our neighbor, we will also work hard at changing the systems that limit and oppress our neighbors. Individual opportunities depend upon group processes and conditions. Reality is like that. Benevolence is not only a matter of helping nice old ladies across the street or of being friends with a few persons of other races. This is not a matter of politicians merely making the best of the old rules. This is a matter of new systems which will end war and racism and poverty and alienation and despair. If we simply heal wounds and do nothing to stop the inflicting of wounds, our action is profoundly immoral, since we have not given the best possible service to our fellow human beings.

Unconventional creativity is a way of contributing to the ongoing process making for good which is seen as a transcendent dimension of all reality. This dynamic release of potentialities goes far beyond the kind of pious prayer that leaves all the grueling sweat to God. Some people intrigued by aspects of the personal devotional life float along with glowing faces, oblivious to the tragedies and ambiguities of life. With eyes fixed on the farthest corner of an anticipated heaven, they do not seem to see things in between such as poor farmers in Chile or subtle race discrimination in their own neighborhood. We all need to remember that we cannot pray very well while we are squeezing the neck of a blameless fellow human being.

In the fierce urgency of our times, those committed to creativity act with assiduous audacity. They are achievement-oriented, not in a compulsive sense or with personal ambition but in a purposive sense of deep caring for suffering persons. They work energetically, strategize systematically, live cheaply, contribute their savings constructively, not for trifling luxuries, but for the achievement of peace, justice, and opportunity for all persons everywhere. They know that to do nothing is now to become an accomplice of injustice and exploitation. To do less than they might do is to contribute to the defeat of their own cause. There are contemporary counterparts to reputable Germans sitting on their hands and muting their voices while Hitler was coming to power.

Some creative persons will concentrate their efforts at one or two points—as on the family and on world peace, or on volunteer tutoring the underprivileged along with a socially productive paid job. Other equally creative persons can effectively spread their efforts over a somewhat wider area, perhaps moving from one to another emphasis over a period of years. At least in minor ways, like writing congressmen or making contributions, all of us can have some influence at every major point of public policy decision.[56] Whatever number of intensive campaigns we may take on, maximum effectiveness suggests three criteria for selection. All of us need to concentrate on what we have thoughtfully determined to be the most fundamental, the most urgent, and the most neglected issues before us.

Creativity has implications both vocationally and avocationally. Our choice of a job or the emphasis we make within our daily work has important social consequences. Outside normal working hours we also have discretion over larger amounts of time which can be used more or less constructively. With four-day workweeks for many, and more three-day holiday weekends for all, we can set some boundaries to goofing off. It is even becoming possible for larger numbers of people to have a double career, the second career being that of a social change agent in direct service to the community. For reasons included in the next chapter much avocational action can most effectively be directed through the church.

Ordinary people in mass society may become decisively involved in the democratic process. While specialized technical competence is necessary administratively to implement decisions, general directions for policy can still be voted at the bottom. During a recent crucial political campaign, a popular lapel button was quite accurate. The inscription could apply to alert homemakers, activist young people, or industrial workers quite amateur to politics. It said, "I'm a Grass Root." In more classical terms, Pericles said of Athens: "We do not regard a man who takes no interest in public affairs as harmless. We do not say that such a man minds his own business. Rather we say he has no business here at all."

An ecstatic actualization of personal powers realistically directed toward important social needs is the clear teaching of the best in religion. Holiness is not quietism or privatism or withdrawal. It is, rather, prophetic contemplation or meditative activism. It is rhapsodic growth joined to ethical zeal. It is mysticism plus militance.

If book titles could be longer, I would have added a third motif for a religion of the future, and would have spoken of reality, ecstasy, and creativity. Based on solidly grounded views of the whole of reality, exploration of the possibilities in religious experience and ecstasy may turn out to be one of the two most exciting adventures of the years ahead. If we act adequately, the other will be participation in remarkable new achievements in social justice and opportunity. Some will feel that the message of this book reduces the content of religion too much by criticizing methods I have called unreliable, historical beliefs considered outdated, or moralisms found oversimple. Far from being reductionist, the three motifs I have developed greatly expand the claim of religion. They provide a more convincing ground for faith, relate belief more pervasively to all that exists, present more thoroughgoing demands over a wider range of life, and make the resources of religion more generously available to larger numbers of those increasingly affected by modern cultural trends.

5

SHOULD WE ABOLISH THE CHURCH?

Is the present-day church an unintentional conspiracy against the religious life? Some think so. They stay out of church not so much because they find religion incredible, but because they find the church incredible. Churches should be radiating excitement and truth. Some people see them as dull, hypocritical hiding places from happiness. There is so much wrong with the church that it sometimes looks as though we had better scrap it and start over.

This conclusion might follow even though we accepted evidence for the unique contribution of religion that has kept appearing throughout this book. By relating the whole of reality to the whole of our existence, religion should lead us to more valid conclusions, since it takes into account a

more comprehensive range of data. It nurtures a
more complete actualization of personal potentialities, providing ecstasy even for those trapped by
circumstance. Its integral emphasis in a highly specialized society helps glue together what is becoming unglued. Religion provides direction and hope
for more thoroughgoing social improvement. Its
guidance for conduct pulls action closer to more
adequate   goals.   Ultimate   concerns   provide
stronger motivation and sources of power beyond
the material and the present. To live with zest and
delight through current threats and opportunities
requires that dimension of reality which includes
the whole and the ultimate.

Recognizing such contributions of religion is not
necessarily concluding that we need a church. Indeed, some would argue that any organization
squeezes the vitality out of the religious impulse.
Or is organization necessary for religious vitality?

Looking Sociological Facts in the Face

Social institutions such as the state, family, economic structures, and the church may be defined
as established patterns of roles and actions, or as
organized and established structures and processes
for satisfying important human needs. There are
basic needs in human groups for order and for the
enforcement of common agreements. Therefore,
societies have developed political institutions.
There are essential needs for food and material
support for life, requiring an economic institution.
So also religious needs would seem to call for cor-

responding structures. As Michael Novak has observed, "Institutions are not so much man's enemy as his natural habitat." [57]

Certain liabilities and dangers always go along with organization. Paying bills and preserving buildings may absorb so much attention that the purposes which the structure was to serve are forgotten or distorted. This kind of goal displacement allows the means to become the end. Therefore the original purpose is never achieved. If such an organization paints the label "church" on its bulletin board, it is engaging in fraudulent advertising.

The primary reason for the church's existence is not to build sanctuaries or to organize committees. Rather, in the words of H. Richard Niebuhr, the basic purpose is "the increase among men of the love of God and neighbor." [58] It is not the church's care for the personally distressed or campaigns for social justice that require explanation. It is, rather, accumulated property and bureaucracy that carry the burden of proof. Does the money and energy spent contribute genuinely to the materially or spiritually poor? It may or may not, depending on whether the service thereby becomes more efficient.

Organizations may also lead to impersonalization, making routine what should be individualized. They may require conformity by all when this is less suitable for some. Or the conformity required may be too heavily conditioned by the past. Institutions easily become conservative, perpetuating the customs of the fathers beyond the deadline for finding better ways.

Fortunately these dangers can be avoided. It is possible to use means functionally. In fact, ends cannot be achieved without means. We now also have enough knowledge about social organizations that developing an institution does not inevitably lead to a decline of spontaneity and intimacy. Institutional structures are not in themselves dehumanizing. On the contrary they are the necessary setting for humanization. Structures may negate the purposes for which they were established. They may also implement those purposes if they are functionally oriented and dynamically motivated.

Those who too easily criticize institutions should consider several reasons for their being indispensable in any large society. For one thing, organized groups are necessary to provide channels for effective communication in mass society. Religion, like other social values, is something to be shared. There are changes to be produced, converts to be won. In a day of competing mass communication, gurus in the woods are not enough to do what must be done. The airwaves seem filled by those who have nothing to say and keep on repeating it. We need a "Sesame Street for grown-ups," Shana Alexander's name for the televised Watergate hearings.[59] The power of mass media, along with other social pressures, needs to be matched by effective religious communication. This kind of publicity requires specialists and a division of labor—in short, organization.

There has been a conspiracy of silence about religion much more serious than the silence about sex. In public conversation we do not easily mention our religious beliefs, worship experiences, or spiritual motivations for conduct. As once we would never speak of masturbation or vasectomies, so we still do not say, "I had a good meditation period this morning," or "I'm doing this because I think God is calling me." Our hang-ups about sex blocked communication about one important though limited social relationship. What is almost a taboo against serious public conversation about religion blacks out discussion of the most important dimension in all of reality.

A second essential reason for a church is to provide a community of support for a new identity. People need anchors in a stormy world. A few bold spirits may continue on course in isolated independence, but most of us need support systems—social groups to reinforce our beliefs and best intentions. Such larger group support becomes especially important for those standing ahead of society, challenging immoralities accepted by the majority—and that is what religion involves.

In the third place, institutions are also essential for adopting sound programs. The give-and-take of group dialogue becomes creatively productive of superior insights. On complex issues we need the contribution of specialists who know enough to guide us on details, and we need organized ways for all the little men affected by decisions to shape general policy. For anyone to insist that he can be a sufficiently knowledgeable Christian without going to something like a church is like saying that he can be an effective statesman without advisers,

or the head of a large business corporation without
a staff.

A fourth reason for institutions is to secure
power to carry out widespread programs such as
those involving social change. In any society larger
than a crossroads hamlet, there is no social action
unless it is organized action. This is especially true
in a democratic society. To accomplish major
ends—whether they be gasoline for motorcycles,
salt for food, or religious curricula for children—we
need to coordinate many different factors. Immediately this requires structural forms. Furthermore,
organization increases effective leverage. Pete
Seeger used Alex Comfort's lyrics to remind us that
neither one man's strength nor even that of two
men can "set the people free, but if two and two
and fifty make a million," freedom can be won.
Any schoolboy knows that mathematically this is
untrue. Sociologically it is an accurate calculation.
An individual alone is powerless. We cannot exert
sufficient social influence without joining organizations. How is one to get a bill passed or a war
stopped? The more one stresses mission or purpose, the more important will functional institutional structures become. As Macquarrie put it,
"Mission and organization depend on one another." [60]

There can now be no adequate social achievements without institutions. To argue otherwise is
to exhibit sociological illiteracy. Destroying institutions in order to preserve their purposes is like
destroying a Vietnamese village in order to save its
life. If we did not have an existing church, we

would have to organize one. Homes, schools, factories, and psychiatrists' offices are not quite all the buildings we need. If there is any future worth having, there will be a church in the middle of society.

Are There Alternatives to Present Churches?

It is not a question of whether we will have religious institutions. Our choice is what kind of religious institutions and how open to constructive change they will be. Even though some sort of religious institution is an essential part of any viable culture, this does not necessarily mean the continuance of the church in its present form. Perhaps the existing church should be replaced by some other organization for the same general purpose. As one possibility, other existing institutions might conceivably take over religious functions.

Of course this would not eliminate all our difficulties. It must honestly be admitted that all social institutions have serious limitations. For economic organizations one could compile a long list of false aims, poor products, and dishonest practices. Political life is notorious for corruption and inefficiency. Family life is marred by divorce, conflict, and irresponsibility. Schools are often dull and irrelevant, or they fail with some children.

Yet all this is a very one-sided picture. It is not an accurate evaluation of the institutions involved. We make changes within these organized groups, but we do not scrap them. Even after a drastic revolution much remains the same. There are still cabinet ministers and local governments, factories and retail outlets. Nor do we move to abolish democracy when the percentage of voters drops. Rather, we put on a drive to get out the vote.

The same caution applies also to negative feelings about the church. To overreact simply because there are imperfections is a kind of sabotage that can destroy society and leave persons lonely, disgruntled, and ineffectual. We had better become *more* active in organizations that are ailing in order to help actualize their unrealized potentialities. When the church as a spiritual reality becomes also a social institution, it becomes subject to all the finite limitations that human frailties impose. But it is also by this incarnation that it becomes possible to relate the resources of religion to existing life. This is one of the facts of life for all social organizations.

A frequent meditation on a rainy Sunday morning might begin by listing all kinds of weaknesses in the worship service as reasons for nonattendance. The case could be made to sound very convincing, especially if the blankets were warm and one had been out late the night before. But the meditation cannot end there and claim any validity. One would have to recall that exactly the same kind of case can be made against attending any inconvenient meeting of the school board, or a college class, or a political club. In none of these cases will the quality of the session be phenomenal. Nothing earthshaking is likely to happen at any single meeting. Therefore, one might stop attendance at meetings—but this would also stop the education of children and personal growth and the political process.

Even given the imperfections of all institutions, could we still advantageously transfer to other agencies functions now performed by the church? This might be comparable to abolishing schools and dividing the educational function among the family, apprenticeship programs in industry, and specialized citizenship-training projects provided by government. One could argue for this because of the defects of modern education, especially if one overlooked its achievements. But such a transfer of school functions would eliminate the possibility of reinforcement within a unified, coherent curriculum, or of dealing with the student as a total person. The use of untrained nonspecialists would reduce standards. For example, relying on parents as teachers would usually mean a poor job on the history of civilization or recent psychological research. Such a restructuring would subordinate the educational function, tending to make it the handmaiden of other interests.

The chief nominees as replacements for the church all have similar inherent limitations for taking over the religious function. Schools provide exploration into truth, and very marginally into the meaning of the whole. But they do not consider it their basic function to provide worship, nor to invite dedication of total life, nor to organize campaigns for political and social change. The mass media say much to many people, but they tend to be shaped by the economically or politically powerful, instead of specializing in discovering the will of God for their programming. Since they must attract the masses in order to survive, they are pressed toward least-common-denominator interpretations. This is much different from authentic religion that becomes the confronting vanguard within society. The state might sponsor a civil religion celebrating the best in national heritage, but, for reasons discussed earlier in this book, authentic religion always exposes the inadequacies of prevailing civil religion. This requires an independent agency separate from political or economic sponsorship. Families have important religious functions, but they can neither provide specialized services nor larger group support. An extension of counseling clinics could include ethical as well as personality problems. Welfare agencies might well handle the physical relief of human suffering. Social-reform organizations can concentrate on structural change. All these still leave to the church the guidance and support which emerge from religious devotions and a comprehensive theological view of reality. To expect another institution to perform the full religious function is like going to the beauty parlor for auto repairs. In integrating a holistic and ultimate dimension with all of life, the church has many critics but no rivals.

The church aims to produce the persons of integrity and the social climate necessary for keeping all other groups at their best. As a matter of realistic social fact, those interested in other institutions should rush to support the church also, since it can uniquely provide the most solid foundations for their work.

What Kind of Church for the Future?

It is quite clear that some existing churches are not now fulfilling their distinctive functions. The evaluation question might be phrased: When is a church not a church? Religious organizations have frequently suffered from chronic amnesia about their purposes. Forgetting the function they set out to perform, they have used up energy and budgets in preparing to do a job they never quite got around to doing. This is like a family going on a week's vacation and spending seven days in the service station filling the gas tank. Finding significant personal and social change a painful or controversial matter, the church has sometimes denied its own ideals in hypocrisy or compromise.

Any church true to its purposes will take seriously its prophetic role. If a distinctive reason for the church's existence is to shape persons and society toward transcendent unrealized possibilities, then to identify the church completely with what exists is a death blow. Any important personal or social change inevitably produces resistance and controversy. Yet any organization intending to shape the future must speak especially on controversial issues. They define the points at which society may change direction significantly. Afraid to give leadership at these turning points, churches have again and again become trivial, trite, and timorous in their message. They no longer have a major reason for existence. All that is left are the services of a country club aspiring to easy levels of decency and a few superficial service projects. It is only a question of time until people discover that other organizations can supply these limited wants more entertainingly than can the church. When major social changes inevitably come about, a church identified with past injustices is discredited and deserted. Reflecting the *status quo* may bring some short-run gains in church membership, but at the expense of long-run collapse. Such a perversion of program is treason from within the church, which is considerably more damaging than attack from outside.

On the other hand, churches have acted courageously from considerably higher motives than self-preservation. Lives have been remarkably changed. Millions of persons have been enabled to cope creatively with serious personal and social crises. Church members have given sacrificially to relief and development projects. Church groups were among the very first to speak on such unpopular and controversial matters as welfare legislation, the right of labor to organize, racial discrimination, economic assistance to developing nations, political extremism, or a new China policy. Considerable skill in mobilizing the "conscience constituency" was demonstrated by church groups in such matters as United States membership in the United Nations and passage of the Civil Rights Act of 1964, both of which may be marked by future historians as major turning points in modern history.

Religion can continue to be a prime source of social activism. Robert Coles tells of a black field hand in Mississippi who told him: "The college

students, they say that the churches dull you and
make you feel satisfied with the way things are.
But I don't think they've ever read their Bible.
They killed our Lord Jesus for fighting against the
big people. . . . What keeps our hopes going, what
inspires us, what we believe in—that's what
church is all about." [61]

If one listens, it is easy to hear lethargic snores
and reactionary snorts inside the church. But without listening very intently at all, one can also hear
the shouts of the prophets of all ages, the hammer-
ing of nails on Calvary, the pounding of pavements
by the shoes of precinct workers inspired by their
faith, the words of Martin Luther King, Jr., to his
congregation on Christmas, 1967: "I have a dream
that one day men will rise up and come to see that
they are made to live together as brothers. . . . It
will be a glorious day, the morning stars will sing
together, and the sons of God will shout for joy."
That too is the church—and this is the appropriate
church for the future.

Another weakness correctly attributed to many
churches is that they look too much to the past in a
society that needs to be future-oriented. For one
thing, church persons have often been hung up on
trivial and outdated moralisms. They fail to see, for
example, that sexuality can today be expressed in
some different ways that are still consistent with
religious norms, or that law and order may even be
enhanced by a review of some legislation about
"crimes without victims," or that considerable cultural pluralism is a good thing. On the other hand,
there has been a dynamic drive about religion that

has led the church again and again to cut through
to basic matters and to stay well ahead of the rest
of society in updating its descriptions of morality.
This has made the church at its best a bridgehead
of sanity and the vanguard of the future.

Many preachers are justifiably charged with
somnambulantly mouthing dull anachronisms,
with no sensitivity to current conditions. There is
no excuse for making dull and forbidding anything
that is as relevant as religion. The religious message is excitingly full of drama, poetry, and music.
It deals with the insecurities of youth, the loneli-
ness and happiness of women, the discour-
agements and triumphs of men, upheavals in the
earth, death and destiny, the crash of doom, and
the dawn of hope. Many churches have seen this
and have been very busy about demonstrating the
contemporary meaning of a historical religion.

One of the most popular theological topics today
is a theology of the future. As Harvey Cox has put
it, "The starting point for any theology of the
church today must be a theology of social
change." [62] There is a self-corrective element in
religion that often makes the church the easiest of
all social institutions to change. When the transcendent elements in theology are taken seriously,
this does for the church even more than a top-
notch department of research and development
does for a manufacturing firm. It leads to an un-
usually critical judgment of imperfections and a
powerful impulse toward renovation.[63] Viewed in
its entirety, the church may now be updating more
effectively than any other social institution.

Witness prophetic activities of the World Council of Churches, Vatican II, experimental ministries, research in religion and health, and new forms for religious experience and social activism. Certainly more of the church has a more forward-looking program for more of society than does any other major social institution.

A church for the future will also provide comfort, support, and care for individuals. Here again, much of the church can be charged with being exactly the opposite: a vast, impersonal aggregation with cold, forbidding relationships. There is too much of this, but with the multiplication of growth groups and relationship training, churches are also manifesting their heritage of love. Many congregations are big enough to have power in influencing decision-making agencies in the larger society, and at the same time they provide a network of small circles of intimacy and warmth within the larger membership. As Andrew Greeley summarizes, "The sociological study of large organizations has at least proceeded far enough to be able to assert not merely that large institutions can sustain small intimate groups within their boundaries, but even that the maintenance of these groups is positively conducive to—indeed, imperative for—the health of the large organization." [64]

One of the more intriguing explorations among alert church persons today is into the possibilities of the church as commune. Through small groups within the larger whole, whether residential or not, churches can provide the important values of communes at their best, such as group support for an alternate life-style (which religious faith always calls for), caring in times of crises, group involvement in social action, intimate nurture of personality formation, and more intense experiences of worship. Why should not church-related college dormitories and retirement homes become such communes in an even fuller sense than a congregation can?

At the same time that the church is condemned for its bigness, it is also criticized for being a helpless minority in the larger society. Again this is not the whole truth. As has been pointed out above, the church has had notable successes. However, in the sense of having its full prescription accepted, the church will always be a distinguished failure. That is part of its distinctive contribution, to stand ahead of the programs others are ready to adopt. Anyone fighting for unpopular causes can expect to lose more elections than he or she wins. The innovator always counts on winning only the last one. One reason churches fail is that they succeed in their mission of attempting a great deal. As Monica Furlong puts it, "They fail because they try, which is a very different and much nobler failure than the failure which results from inertia." [65]

We deserve the whole truth about the church. A large part of what is called the church is dead already. It has not genuinely been the church for some time. But other parts of the church are very much alive. As a social organization, the church has been given unfair treatment in modern literature, drama, and supposedly sophisticated conversation. Oversimplification has painted a caricature.

Unfortunate personal experiences have been universalized, or attempts have been made to handle one's own fears or guilt feelings by psychological projection on the church. When the worst features have been presented as the entire picture, the most glorious chapters in the history and present life of the church have been omitted.

At least it must be said that in terms of its continuously effective influence on persons and society in the direction of unattained goals, the church is, in Robert K. Hudnut's phrase, a "sleeping giant." The church is the biggest voluntary organization in the world. It has representatives in every country of the world, and a meeting place and paid staff in practically every neighborhood and village in our land. It is the only organization that brings together its members for what might be called a worldwide meeting every week. The church is the most revolutionary organization in the world, calling for a more comprehensive and a deeper change in both individuals and society than any revolutionary party.[66] What could such a church do if thoroughly awakened?

Unity Among Churches and World Religions?

The potential strength of religious organizations is even greater when they develop cooperation or unity. Churches have often been criticized for remaining narrow and becoming fragmented into separate denominations and faiths. It is true that some groups would rather split than switch, even on insignificant details. But again there is a larger truth. The ecumenical movement toward church unity is one of the most significant facts of our time.

There is considerable misunderstanding about the meaning of unity. Ecumenism carries two emphases, inclusive cooperation and dynamic authenticity. On the one hand, their common emphasis on love and reconciliation leads religious groups to express deep fellowship and mutual support. On the other hand, all vital religious groups are probing mystery, with constantly new discoveries of God's nature and purposes. This leads to genuine differences that need to be authentically expressed both in group action and in intergroup dialogue. A more advanced consensus becomes possible only as all state their cases as frankly and as persuasively as possible in serious interaction. By the very nature of the case, ecumenism therefore always involves unity in diversity.

This is often overlooked by those who urge the merger of churches into one great church with such an emphasis on a common creed, a form of worship, and a general program as to make diversity difficult. Pushing structural unification to this extent would be just as bad as a business monopoly or as a single autocratic world state that would enforce cultural conformity without any balance of power. While some church mergers are undoubtedly wise, the best overall approach to ecumenical unity may well prove to be through councils of churches that allow both joint impact on common emphases and subsidiary group expression of diverse positions.

On this matter churches have been unnecessarily masochistic in self-blame, while critics of the church have exaggerated the problem of fragmentation. In such bodies as the National Council of Churches and the World Council of Churches a substantial part of the church is already unified. Some additional churches with a sufficiently similar emphasis should still join such councils, and members should transfer to such councils some additional functions on which common action is possible. Within Christendom this may be the most significant expression of the ecumenical spirit in the decades ahead.

The next century is also likely to bring an expansion of the ecumenical spirit beyond Christendom to include other major world religions. We need to overcome institutional provincialism and theological ethnocentrism just as we have already attacked a similar spirit in racial prejudice. More than ever before, we now recognize truth in other religious traditions. In the past many were afraid to admit this, since it would seem to weaken the claim of their own religion. That was a tragic mistake. Quite the opposite is true. If the only persons to come to the conclusions embodied in our faith were those in the Judeo-Christian tradition, and if the experience of the rest of the world through its long history led to different conclusions, then our reading of God's reality might well be at fault. To the extent that there is agreement between religions of the world, we can have greater confidence in their teachings. It is when scientists replicate experiments or as agreement emerges among historians that we especially accept their conclusions.

We are too much walled in as we limit ourselves
to our Middle Eastern or European past. Peter
Berger soundly observed, "It is healthy for nuns to
have to deal with rabbis, and vice versa, and it
won't hurt either group to come up against a few
Hindu holy men." [67] The notion that God revealed
himself only through the Christian tradition is both
too low a view of God and too high a view of persons in our tradition. If God withheld himself from
all except the Jews and their successors, then God
is arbitrary, unjust, and immoral. Our own tradition
insists that it is the nature of a loving God to give
himself to all men generously and actively. There
are Biblical roots for saying of God that in all the
nations "as the bountiful Giver he did not leave
himself without a witness" (Acts 14:17, Moffatt).
Differences in knowledge of God are due not to
God's hiding himself but to varying degrees of responsive openness among men. But it would be
strange indeed and contrary to all experience if the
responsive saints and seers were all confined to
one race or nationality or culture. The persons we
know are not good enough to allow us to hold a
discriminatory view of other groups. Some individuals of other religious faiths have excelled many in
the Judeo-Christian tradition. A bigoted, racist, na-
tionalist Christian needs conversion considerably
more than does a sensitive, benevolent, spiritually
aware Hindu or Buddhist. Attributing innate inferi-
ority to whole peoples resident in other parts of the
world is manifestly false social science, just as
viewing God as playing favorites with a "chosen

people" is very poor theology.

Other major world faiths are not so inferior that all their elements must be completely displaced. Nor is it enough to adopt the pallid and dull syncretism that Peter Berger described as a "theological Esperanto" [68] or that Harvey Cox called "universal pabulum." [69] Simply collecting interesting religious specimens into a kind of philosophical Noah's ark is not a rich enough unity. Instead, each religion can find in other religions some things that are valid and that it can incorporate without doing violence to the unity of its own essential faith. Often there are already roots for the new emphasis in neglected strands of one's own religious tradition which can be brought from obscurity and given greater prominence. There are still genuinely different points of view among world faiths. These cannot be considered equally adequate. But there is enough agreement to sustain dialogue out of which increasing convergence can emerge. All would then benefit from the best in each. This process has already occurred when religions confronted other sources of knowledge about reality. The Judeo-Christian tradition was reconceived in confronting Greco-Roman civilization and modern science. Even greater enrichment may lie ahead for all world religions as they receptively encounter each other in what is an increasingly common world environment.

Developing cooperation on common projects will require a world council of religions, much as we have international agencies for governments or sciences. The limited but significant functions of

an overall council of the world's religions might
include facilitating dialogue that is genuine, rather
than soliloquy in disguise. It could also administer
joint campaigns on social issues of common interest. Major world religions are allies against secularism and materialism, against war and selfishness
and exploitation. Theirs is a common cause against
threatening night when the world stands on the
brink of nuclear and ecological annihilation.

What to Do till the Millennium Comes

In all the areas suggested in preceding pages,
the church mixes weakness and strength. As we
come to see the church as indispensable, we support the church, as we do other important social organizations, for what it might be as well as for what
it is. We continue to live in a nation—and even to
live with ourselves—for the same reason. No nation and no one of us is perfectly attractive at any
given moment. We work with both to actualize potentialities.

If many of us were to set down our dream for the
church of our choice, it would include a church
that remembers its reason for being and subordi-
nates bureaucratic activity to higher loyalties; a
church whose beliefs go beyond superstition to a
firm grounding in reality—a vaster, more inspiring
view of God that does not contradict other knowledge but that adds meaning, assurance, and power
to all our knowing; a church actualizing the full
human potentiality in a new life beyond our dreary
mediocrity, and vital ecstatic experience beyond

customary "highs"; a church that adds to our Biblical and theological heritage an emphasis on the findings of the physical and behavioral sciences in a message conveying concrete help on currently existing problems—a positive, hopeful, future-oriented approach emphasizing the continual presence of the living Spirit of truth instead of assuming a completed revelation; a church not defensive or imperialistic with respect to other religions, but uniting in exploration toward deeper discovery and more powerful cooperation; a church more caring in its intimate group relationships, more profound in its education, and more effective in action moving beyond verbalization to the relief of suffering and the fashioning of greatly improved structures for society.

Having fantasized about this kind of church that we could be enthusiastic about, we return to reality to find that it is already here in the process of building. The question then becomes, Will we build as well as dream? We can become more hopeful about the possibilities of the church when we become more helpful within the church.

The millennium, in the sense of the golden age of a responsive church, has not yet arrived. Therefore, we need a practical postscript to this book. If persons honestly think it tragic that the church is not all it should be, then they will think it important to join and to change the church. But doing that is not as simple as saying it. In view of the vast difficulties of such a project, four suggestions may help.

First, join a local congregation which is close to

your conviction or comparatively open to change. Some churches have more positive possibilities than others. One person barely hanging on to the edges of the church came to the climax of his pilgrimage when he could say with enthusiasm, "I had given up on church till I found yours." Some discouraged in their youth or a decade ago have not kept up with the great changes in some leading churches. Change in some churches, like recent change in other aspects of life, has been so rapid that without contact during the last two or three years, we may not know what is going on. Remembering a dreary background, a visitor at a summer intergenerational project in a progressive church exclaimed: "Wow, this isn't Sunday school! This is learning!"

It may well be that some persons ought to stay with churches that are reluctant to change in order to bring them slowly along. Those who are more radically discontented will look for the congregations that are more open to rapid improvement and have the most creative leadership. Often a forward-looking minister or lay group within such a church is eagerly seeking allies in progress.

A second possible way to improve experience within an imperfect church is to concentrate on the most meaningful activities in the congregation of your choice. To a considerable extent it is possible to do one's own thing within a somewhat inhospitable whole. Again, this is what people do in other organizations when they accept one committee assignment and decline others. Or even if one hates San Diego (but who would?), he or she may still love the Point Loma section. A rich offering of diverse emphases has been made possible historically by *ecclesiolae in ecclesia,* or smaller groups within the larger church. A person with a heavy concern for social action can now become a member of a committee charged with that responsibility. If meditation seems promising, it does not take many persons to form a group and experience the power waiting to be so released. The possibility of semiautonomous task forces now extends the range of pluralism within a single congregation. Such groups may use church facilities and be a part of the total program, but act only in their own name without officially committing the church. Again and again large-scale change has begun with these various types of subunits.

A third individual approach for anyone who expects to contribute to change in the church is to exert more fully influence in overall congregational decisions. Like any other organization, local churches are run by a "clique," if we mean by "clique" a smaller number who are disproportionately active and occupy positions of leadership. But church leadership is usually surprisingly open. It is likely to welcome with open arms a dedicated and reasonably attractive person willing to put in time and effort. The governing board may seem to be loaded with do-nothing types who consider "don't rock the boat" to be the best way to get "full steam ahead." Changing the character of governing boards means developing candidates, increasing support for new ideas so that they deserve representation, and using skill in working with the selection process. This requires persistence and co-operation. Often the people who are strong on vision and insight are soft on strategy.

One wins influence in organizations as he or she supports acceptable existing programs with initiative and imagination. Any group has a right to expect a demonstration of commitment to basic goals, which are valued by the group, and competence in helping achieve those goals. When one has effectively taught long hours in the church school, his or her suggestions for improving educational programs are taken more seriously. Influence also assumes speaking out relevantly and persuasively when decisions are to be made. To contribute to the future of the organization, those who have walked out of churches need to walk back in again, attend more regularly, and work more actively.

To expand the promise of the church, a fourth suggestion is to expect to be changed yourself. Revitalization of the religious institution will take more insight and skill than anyone of us has. The best way is surely in some respects different from what I now advocate. We need to learn from each other and from God. There is always danger that any small group of people with a prescription for church reformation may become self-centered, prideful, and dogmatic. Safeguards can be found in sincere cultivation of personal devotional practices, openness to new evidence, and encouragement of opposition expression. As we so strengthen democratic processes, the church becomes less likely to stone its prophets, among which we would like to include ourselves.

I have been contending that because of its all-inclusive and profound effects, the single greatest imperative during the decades ahead is recovery of a religious life-style, rooted in reality and releasing the ecstasy of full actualization of personal and social potential. For this enterprise we have abundant resources. This book has provided clues to many of them. We can positively assert the essence of religious faith and ways to relate it to the world. Yet building an intellectual case or communicating ideas is not enough. Emotional support, personal commitment, and accepting the divine beyond in our midst are also essential. These each of us must provide.

What the average person is now doing in a political party will not save the nation. What the average person is now doing in the church will not save the world. But what may be initiated by an aware and active minority in close relationship with God can save the world. Majority action has always first been minority commitment. That initial impetus requires courage and initiative. The most fundamental point of thrust is religious in nature. This is the indispensable ingredient to add to all our being and doing. There is no substitute for change in one's own way of life—for beginning to meditate and keeping it up over a long enough period of time, for joining a selected church and taking leadership responsibility, for becoming active in community decision. There really is no substitute for whatever is the first step in the process for you—revising your engagement calendar or starting the motor of your car. There really is no substitute.

NOTES

1. Rocco Caporale and Antonio Grumelli (eds.), *The Culture of Unbelief* (University of California Press, 1971), p. 1.

2. *Newsweek*, October 29, 1973, p. 67.

3. Theodore Roszak, *Where the Wasteland Ends: Politics and Transcendence in Post-Industrial Society* (Doubleday & Company Inc., 1972), p. 203.

4. Rudolf Bultmann in Hans Bartsch (ed.), *Kerygma and Myth* (London: S.P.C.K., 1953), p. 5.

5. Dietrich Bonhoeffer, *Letters and Papers from Prison*, ed. by Eberhard Bethge, tr. by Reginald H. Fuller (London: SCM Press, Ltd., 1953), p. 124.

6. Heinz Zahrnt, *The Question of God* (Harcourt Brace Jovanovich, Inc., 1969), pp. 240–241.

7. Peter Berger, *A Rumor of Angels* (Doubleday & Company, Inc., 1969), p. 65.

8. Roszak, *op. cit.*, p. 306.

9. Paul Tillich, *Theology of Culture* (Oxford University Press, 1959), p. 41.

10. Harold K. Schilling, *The New Consciousness in Science and Religion* (United Church Press, 1973), p. 26.

11. Martin Buber, *I and Thou* (Edinburgh: T. & T. Clark, 1937), pp. 6–8.

12. Roger Garaudy, *From Anathema to Dialogue: A Marxist Challenge to the Christian Churches*, tr. by Luke O'Neill (Herder & Herder, Inc., 1966), p. 110.

13. Arnold J. Toynbee, abridg. by D. C. Somervell, *A Study of History* (Oxford University Press, 1947), Chs. 5–8.

14. Berger, *op. cit.*, p. 75.

15. Henry Nelson Wieman, *The Source of Human Good* (The University of Chicago Press, 1946).

16. Pierre Teilhard de Chardin, *The Divine Milieu* (Harper & Brothers, 1960), p. 31.

17. John B. Cobb, Jr., *God and the World* (The Westminster Press, 1969), p. 45.

18. E. Schillebeeckx, *God: The Future of Man* (Sheed & Ward, Inc., 1968), p. 181.

19. Harvey Cox in Daniel Callahan (ed.), *The Secular City Debate* (The Macmillan Company, 1966), p. 203.

20. John Macquarrie, *God and Secularity* (The Westminster Press, 1967), p. 108.

21. Paul Tillich, *Systematic Theology* (The University of Chicago Press, 1951), Vol. I, p. 223.

22. John B. Cobb, Jr., *A Christian Natural Theology* (The Westminster Press, 1965), p. 39.

23. Leroy T. Howe, *Prayer in a Secular World* (Pilgrim Press, 1973), p. 150.

24. John A. T. Robinson, *Honest to God* (The Westminster Press, 1963), pp. 48–49.

25. Tillich, *Theology of Culture*, p. 132.

26. Georgia Harkness, *Conflicts in Religious Thought* (Henry Holt & Company, Inc., 1929), p. 319.

27. "Atomic Warfare and the Christian Faith: Report of the Commission on the Relation of the Church to the War in the Light of the Christian Faith" (Federal Council of Churches, 1946), p. 5.

28. Reinhold Niebuhr, *The Nature and Destiny of Man* (Charles Scribner's Sons, 1941), Vol. I, p. 122.

29. John Macquarrie, *Three Issues in Ethics* (Harper & Row, Publishers, Inc., 1970), p. 122.

30. Ernest Cadman Colwell, *Approach to the Teaching of Jesus* (Abingdon-Cokesbury Press, 1946), p. 81.

31. W. Norman Pittenger, "Toward a More Christian Theology," *Religion in Life,* Winter 1967, p. 504.

32. Berger, *op. cit.,* p. 35.

33. C. S. Lewis, *Surprised by Joy: The Shape of My Early Life* (Harcourt, Brace & Co., Inc., 1956).

34. Paul Tillich, *The Protestant Era* (The University of Chicago Press, 1948), p. 267.

35. Roszak, *op. cit.,* pp. 16, 18.

36. Erik H. Erikson, *Gandhi's Truth* (W. W. Norton & Company, Inc., 1969), p. 399.

37. Sue Reilley, "Dr. Glasser Without Failure," *Human Behavior,* May 1973, p. 18.

38. Tillich, *Systematic Theology,* Vol. III, p. 242.

39. James A. Pike, *If This Be Heresy* (Harper & Row, Publishers, Inc., 1967), p. 139.

40. Cobb, *God and the World,* p. 102.

41. *Newsweek,* June 25, 1973, p. 80.

42. Robert L. Johnson, *Counter Culture and the Vision of God* (Augsburg Publishing House, 1971), p. 49.

43. Abraham H. Maslow, *Religions, Values and Peak-Experiences* (Ohio State University Press, 1964), pp. xi–xii.

44. Paul Tillich, "Spiritual Presence," *Union Seminary Quarterly Review,* January 1962, p. 123.

45. Brother Lawrence, *The Practice of the Presence of God,* various editions.

46. Robert N. Bellah, "Civil Religion in America," in Donald R. Cutler (ed.), *The Religious Situation: Nineteen Sixty Eight* (Beacon Press, 1968), pp. 331–356.

47. Robert K. Hudnut, *The Sleeping Giant: Arousing Church Power in America* (Harper & Row, Publishers, Inc., 1971), p. 44.

48. *Concern*, December 15, 1962, pp. 8–9.

49. Harvey Cox, *The Seduction of the Spirit* (Simon & Schuster, Inc., 1973), p. 224.

50. For a more detailed discussion of the preceding problems, see Harvey Seifert, *Ethical Resources for Political and Economic Decision* (The Westminster Press, 1972); John C. Bennett, *Foreign Policy in Christian Perspective* (Charles Scribner's Sons, 1966); Harvey Seifert, *Ethical Resources for International Relations* (The Westminster Press, 1964); John M. Swomley, Jr., *Liberation Ethics* (The Macmillan Company, 1972); Donella H. Meadows *et al.*, *The Limits to Growth: A Report for the Club of Rome's Project on the Predicament of Mankind* (Universe Books, 1972).

51. For an expansion of these general proposals, see sources in preceding note.

52. For a fuller discussion of the weaknesses of contemporary life-styles, see my *Ethical Resources for Political and Economic Decision*, pp. 142–151.

53. Harvey Cox, *The Seduction of the Spirit*, p. 223.

54. Jürgen Moltmann, *Theology of Hope*, tr. by James W. Leitch (Harper & Row, Publishers, Inc., 1967), p. 21.

55. Gustavo Gutiérrez, *A Theology of Liberation*, tr. by Caridad Inda, Sr., and John Eagleson (Orbis Books, 1972), p. 262.

56. See my *Power Where the Action Is* (The Westminster Press, 1968), especially Chs. 4 and 5, for practical suggestions.

57. Michael Novak, *Ascent of the Mountain, Flight of the Dove* (Harper & Row, Publishers, Inc., 1971), p. xii.

58. H. Richard Niebuhr, *The Purpose of the Church and Its Ministry* (Harper & Brothers, 1956), p. 31.

59. *Newsweek*, June 11, 1973, p. 35.

60. John Macquarrie, *An Existential Theology* (Harper & Row, Publishers, Inc., 1965), p. 223.

61. George White, "Psychiatry and Belief: A Conversation with Robert Coles," *Commonweal*, October 27, 1972, pp. 81–82.

62. Harvey Cox, *The Secular City*, rev. ed. (The Macmillan Company, 1966), p. 91.

63. See Paul Tillich's discussion of "the Protestant principle" in *The Protestant Era*, Chs. 11 and 15.

64. Andrew M. Greeley, *Religion in the Year 2000* (Sheed & Ward, Inc., 1969), p. 156.

65. Monica Furlong, *Contemplating Now* (The Westminster Press, 1971), p. 74.

66. Hudnut, *op. cit.*, Ch. 16.

67. Berger, *op. cit.*, p. 99.

68. *Ibid.*, p. 101.

69. Cox, *The Seduction of the Spirit*, p. 151.